OECD Studies on SMEs and Entrepreneurship

Scaling Up Public Financial and Non-Financial Support for SME Sustainability

INNOVATIONS AND GOOD PRACTICES

Please cite this publication as:
OECD (2025), *Scaling Up Public Financial and Non-Financial Support for SME Sustainability: Innovations and Good Practices*, OECD Studies on SMEs and Entrepreneurship, OECD Publishing, Paris, https://doi.org/10.1787/bf835159-en.

ISBN 978-92-64-74552-0 (print)
ISBN 978-92-64-50849-1 (PDF)
ISBN 978-92-64-85073-6 (HTML)

OECD Studies on SMEs and Entrepreneurship
ISSN 2078-0982 (print)
ISSN 2078-0990 (online)

Photo credits: Cover © Sakorn Sukkasemsakorn/Getty Images Plus.

Corrigenda to OECD publications may be found at: https://www.oecd.org/en/publications/support/corrigenda.html.

Foreword

This report analyses good practices in the provision of public financial and non-financial support to facilitate SME greening. By exploring both financing instruments and complementary policy support mechanisms implemented in different countries around the world, the report aims to provide actionable insights for policymakers, including public development banks, SME agencies, multilateral development banks and other stakeholders with similar mandates of providing financial and non-financial support for the green transition of SMEs.

Through a mapping of different types of public financial and non-financial support relevant for SME innovators, enablers and adopters, and a detailed review of case studies, the report showcases practical examples of successful and/or innovative instruments and programmes, including aspects of their design, implementation, and outcomes, as relevant and available. Furthermore, the report synthesises lessons learned from these initiatives aiming to provide insights and guidance for adopting and scaling effective interventions in different country contexts.

This report is part of the OECD Committee on SMEs and Entrepreneurship (CSMEE) Programme of Work and Budget for 2025-26. It advances the work of the OECD Platform on Financing SMEs for Sustainability by identifying good practices to enhance provision and uptake of sustainable finance for SMEs. It builds on and deepens previous CSMEE work on this topic, including the 2022 policy paper on *Financing SMEs for Sustainability Drivers, Constraints and Policies*, as well as the 2023 survey report on *Financial institution strategies and approaches*, which identified the types of financial and non-financial support instruments being deployed for SMEs. It also contributes to the work of the OECD Financing SMEs and Entrepreneurs Scoreboard and to the OECD Horizontal Project on Net Zero+. The report was submitted for comments to the CSMEE on 29 September 2025, under cote CFE/SME(2025)5/REV1.

Acknowledgements

This report was produced by the OECD Centre for Entrepreneurship, SMEs, Regions and Cities (CFE), led by Lamia Kamal-Chaoui, Director, as part of the programme of work of the OECD Committee on SMEs and Entrepreneurship (CSMEE). The development of this report benefited from the inputs of Delegates of the CSMEE, chaired by Angelina Cannizzaro (Department for Business and Trade, United Kingdom), and its Informal Steering Group on SME and Entrepreneurship Financing, as well as the members of the OECD Platform on Financing SMEs for Sustainability.

This publication was written by Marija Kuzmanovic (Policy Analyst, CFE) and Giulia Honegger (Policy Analyst, CFE) under the supervision of Lucia Cusmano (Head of Division, CFE) and Miriam Koreen (Senior Counsellor and Head of Unit, CFE). Kris Boschmans (Senior Researcher, IDEA Consult) contributed to Chapter 5 and the case studies, with the support of Giulia Bergui (Analyst, IDEA Consult). The report also benefited from valuable feedback from Nadim Ahmad (Deputy Director, CFE) and Karen Maguire (Senior Counsellor, CFE). Yoshiyuki Miyoshi (Senior Counsellor, OECD) helped facilitate contacts with financial institutions.

The report was developed with the financial support and inputs of the members of the OECD Platform on Financing SMEs for Sustainability - the British Business Bank, the Business Development Bank of Canada, the Industrial Bank of Korea and Cassa Depositi e Prestiti – whose contributions are gratefully acknowledged.

The report benefited from the valuable inputs provided by participants in the case study consultations, whose insights are gratefully acknowledged: Nattasuda Anusonadisai and Pang Thitirat Sittakaradej (Asian Development Bank), Susan Rohac and William Polushin (The Business Development Bank of Canada), Jussi Åkerberg and Tessa Skinner (Business Finland), Jai Shah and Anjana Seshadri (SBI Ventures Limited), Zakiah Mat Esa, Asmayuzi Ismail and Nanthakumaran Thankamony (SME Bank Malaysia), Amanda Alletorp Edwards (Export and Investment Fund of Denmark), Navina Balasingam, Mishallani Nair Reveendran and Muhammad Al Fadzriq Hamzah (Capital Markets Malaysia), Alina Cebotariov, Vadim Indoitu, Iaroslav Rurac and Vadim Codreanu (The Organization for Entrepreneurship Development), Vivek Kotak (Solar Victoria), Jan Riegl (National Development Bank of the Czech Republic), Anders Bomholdt and Frederik Weiergang Larsen (Danish Business Authority), Kyong Ran Seo, Justin Ham, and So Jeong In (The Industrial Bank of Korea), Karen Garcia Mata Alanis, Jocelyn Alexia Flores Gonzalez, Ivan Vicente Cornejo Villalva and Juan Carlos Freyre (Nacional Financiera), Erik Welin and Rozália Pál (European Investment Bank), Ana Vele, Jana Lorger, Rok Huber, Igor Kotarščak and Tina Zager (Slovenian Enterprise Fund), Adelaide Cracco, Diana Patrascu, Frank Lang, Andrea Hermida Parapar, Lievijne Neuteboom, Ghislain Terrier and Raluca Stanciu (European Investment Fund), Onur Bingöl, Can Saripinarli, Paolo Monaco, Merve Bas and Elif Nalbantoglu Çelebi (The European Bank for Reconstruction and Development), Claren Kwei Fang Chang and Kenneth Foo (DBS Bank), Shen Yang Mok (Enterprise Singapore), Giulio Franci and Kumbirai Makanza (Renewable Energy and Energy Efficiency Partnership), representatives from Shoko Chukin Bank, Marloes van den Berg and Eva Top (Netherlands Enterprise Agency).

Table of contents

Foreword 3

Acknowledgements 4

Executive summary 7

1 Introduction 10
- 1.1. SMEs have a key role to play in the global sustainability agenda 11
- 1.2. Financial and non-financial support are critical for accelerating SME greening 12
- 1.3. Financial and non-financial support needs to be tailored to SMEs' diverse needs and contributions to the green economy 12
- 1.4. References 14

2 SME innovators: Financial and non-financial support mechanisms 16
- 2.1. Financial support for SME innovators 18
- 2.2. Non-financial support for SME innovators 26
- 2.3. References 30

3 SME enablers: Financial and non-financial support mechanisms 34
- 3.1. Financial support for SME enablers 35
- 3.2. Non-financial support for enablers 41
- 3.3. References 42

4 SME adopters: Financial and non-financial support mechanisms 44
- 4.1. Financial support for SME adopters 45
- 4.2. Non-financial support for adopters 59
- References 67

5 Lessons learned and good practices in the provision of financial and non-financial support to SMEs 73
- 5.1. Key trends and features in financial support for SME greening 75
- 5.2. Key lessons learned and factors for success 77
- 5.3. References 83

6 Conclusions 84

Annex A. Case studies 86

Annex B. Glossary 87

TABLES

Table 1.1. SMEs need different support based on their roles in the green transition 14
Table 2.1. Common financial support instruments for SME green innovators 19
Table 2.2. Non-financial support programmes for SME innovators 27
Table 3.1. Common financial support instruments for SME green transition enablers 36
Table 3.2. Non-financial support programmes for SME enablers 41
Table 4.1. Common financial support options for SMEs adopters of green solutions 46
Table 4.2. Common non-financial support programmes for SME adopters 60
Table 5.1. Overview of case studies 74

BOXES

Box 2.1. Examples of direct and indirect financing instruments for green innovators 20
Box 2.2. Examples of equity and quasi equity financing for green innovators 23
Box 2.3. Examples of financial support for innovators delivered through incubators and accelerators 25
Box 2.4. Examples of innovation prizes for green start-ups and innovators 26
Box 2.5. Examples of R&D collaboration programmes 27
Box 2.6. Examples of incubator and accelerator support programmes 28
Box 2.7. Examples of testbeds, pilots and knowledge-sharing platforms for green innovators 29
Box 3.1. Examples of direct and indirect financing instruments for enablers 37
Box 3.2. Examples of risk sharing instruments for enablers 39
Box 3.3. Examples of trade and supply chain financing for enablers 40
Box 3.4. Examples of business development services and market access support programmes for SME enablers 41
Box 4.1. Examples of direct financing instruments for adopters 49
Box 4.2. Examples of risk sharing instruments 53
Box 4.3. Examples of incentive-based instruments 56
Box 4.4. Examples of sustainability-linked instruments for adopters 57
Box 4.5. Examples of green trade finance for adopters 58
Box 4.6. Examples of awareness campaigns and training programmes for SME adopters 61
Box 4.7. Examples of technical assistance programmes for SME adopters 62
Box 4.8. Examples of support with standards and certifications, knowledge sharing networks and peer learning 64
Box 4.9. Tools and support for SME sustainability reporting 65

Executive summary

Many countries are seeking to promote more environmentally friendly and sustainable business practices, particularly for small and medium-sized enterprises (SMEs). Globally, SMEs represent more than 90% of all businesses and account for more than half of total business employment and value added. Their economic weight means that their collective actions can significantly accelerate progress toward sustainability targets. SMEs also hold a pivotal role in reshaping markets and supply chains, making their engagement indispensable for achieving sustainable, resilient and competitive economies.

SMEs and start-ups play multiple roles in the green transition:

- **As innovators**, that develop disruptive green technologies and offer novel solutions to address sustainability challenges;
- **As enablers** that produce and disseminate green products, services and technologies to help other businesses implement sustainable practices;
- **As adopters** that incorporate existing green technologies and processes into their operations to reduce their environmental footprint.

While SMEs share many common challenges in the green transition, their specific needs differ depending upon the role they play (innovator, enabler, adopter). Common challenges include more limited access to finance, awareness, skills and expertise gaps, and disproportionate regulatory and administrative burdens compared to large firms. In terms of the type of SME, innovators often struggle to secure patient, high-risk capital to bring new technologies and solutions to market, and they need advisory and capacity building support on commercialisation, intellectual property management and regulatory compliance. SME enablers require support to expand their operational capacity, integrate into sustainable value chains and access markets that reward green solutions. SME adopters need affordable credit, advisory services and simplified compliance tools to integrate sustainability into their day-to-day operations. Recognising this mix of shared barriers and differentiated needs is essential for designing policies and financing instruments that enable SMEs to fully contribute to sustainability objectives.

The report analyses public support instruments worldwide and in-depth case studies from a range of countries to show how tailored policies and support mechanism can help SME innovators, enablers and adopters to foster the green transition. It documents how traditional instruments are being redesigned or repurposed to serve the sustainability-related financing needs of SMEs, including through green loans, leases, guarantees and other instruments. At the same time, there is increasing recognition that more tailored and flexible instruments may be needed to encourage SMEs to invest in sustainability. The report, thus, also showcases novel instruments like sustainability-linked loans, revenue-based financing or property-linked financing that have been designed to address specific supply- and demand-side constraints, such as high costs, cash flow pressures and collateral requirements. It demonstrates how different blended financing structures and other risk-sharing instruments are being deployed to mobilise private sector financing for green investments. It also provides numerous examples of how financial support can be paired with non-financial support to strengthen the uptake and impact of these instruments

Building on more than 20 case studies, the report also sheds light on practical considerations and lessons learned for the design and implementation of publicly provided financial and non-financial support for SMEs:

Targeting market gaps and mobilising private capital

- **Addressing identified market gaps or externalities:** Public financial support programmes for SME greening should target gaps in private provision, such as in cases where investments are seen as too risky, returns are uncertain or lengthy, or information gaps prevent lenders and firms from making informed decisions. This is relevant for many green investments, where environmental benefits may not be fully priced into markets and where SMEs often face higher upfront costs and longer payback periods.
- **Unlocking private investments:** Private capital is key to achieving scale in financing the green transition. Public funds should therefore be used strategically to crowd in commercial capital. Programmes can achieve this by designing risk-sharing mechanisms that lower perceived risks, streamline procedures to reduce transaction costs for financial intermediaries, and signal market viability for newer sectors and investment types. In the context of green investments, such interventions can be especially powerful in de-risking emerging low-carbon technologies and energy-efficiency measures, where private investors may be hesitant to enter without clear signals of market viability and public co-investment.
- **Supporting commercially viable investments:** Public financial support is most effective when it helps SMEs undertake green projects that can stand on their own commercially, rather than relying indefinitely on subsidies. By de-risking early investments, demonstrating market potential, and crowding in private capital, such interventions can also accelerate the development of viable green business models that can scale.

Enhancing access and effectiveness for SMEs

- **Balancing potential trade-offs between SME access and impact**: Public financial support programmes for SME greening have to navigate the tension between broadening access to smaller or less advanced firms and ensuring measurable, high-quality impact. Setting eligibility and reporting thresholds too high risks excluding many SMEs with significant improvement potential, while lowering them too far can dilute outcomes and stretch administrative capacity. Effective programmes find middle ground by calibrating requirements, streamlining processes, and offering non-financial support so that more firms can participate without compromising credibility or results.
- **Reducing SME compliance costs by aligning processes and reporting with (inter)national standards:** Meeting eligibility criteria and compliance requirements, including through reporting on sustainability-related KPIs, can be very burdensome for SMEs. If these requests are not standardised, this can further exacerbate the compliance burden of SMEs. Public bodies can draw on emerging practices from national administrations and international institutions to standardise templates, align criteria with recognised taxonomies and adopt proportional verification to facilitate SME compliance.
- **Strengthening access and impact through flexibility and adaptability:** Green and sustainability-linked SME financing instruments are still at an early stage of development in many jurisdictions, with best practices only beginning to emerge. Programmes are therefore evolving, as institutions, intermediaries and policymakers gain experience, experiment with different approaches and learn from implementation challenges. This iterative process is essential, as ongoing adjustments allow programmes to better balance access and impact, strengthen monitoring and reporting systems, and refine the mix of financial and non-financial support needed.

Strengthening delivery mechanisms and partnerships

- **Choosing the right intermediaries and partners**: For complex intermediated finance solutions, effective programmes depend on intermediaries with the systems, expertise, and governance needed to implement the programmes effectively and transparently. This is equally relevant for supply-chain financing instruments, where strong partners can aggregate demand, enforce credible standards, and strengthen uptake among SMEs. In the delivery of non-financial support, the selection of capable partners is critical to ensure high-quality advisory services and technical assistance, particularly in areas where public financial institutions lack in-house expertise. Beyond technical capacity, the alignment of partners' incentives with programme objectives is also essential, as is ensuring accountability through clear performance metrics.
- **Leveraging digital tools for access, uptake and efficient implementation:** Use of digital platforms and technologies can facilitate the engagement of both financial intermediaries and SMEs in green and sustainable finance. For intermediaries, digital tools can streamline application processing, automate reporting, and improve monitoring of environmental outcomes, reducing administrative costs and ensuring greater consistency. For SMEs, online portals, self-assessment tools, and simplified digital forms can lower entry barriers, cut compliance burdens, and provide clearer guidance on eligibility and reporting.

Building awareness, capacity and ecosystem support

- **Making outreach an integral part of support:** For many SMEs, sustainability is not yet a strategic priority, and even where it is recognised as important, firms often lack relevant knowledge (e.g. on sustainability gaps, appropriate technolgies and processes to adopt, etc.). Many programmes, therefore, implement systematic outreach efforts to bolster SME awareness and uptake. Non-financial support in the form of checklists, guides, audits, and other interventions (see below) are used to further reinforce outreach efforts by boosting incentives and demand for greening and related financing.
- **Strengthening non-financial support for SME investments in greening and uptake of associated financing:** Financing alone is insufficient for SMEs to access and benefit from green investment programmes, as many SMEs face technical and administrative barriers. Complementary non-financial support—such as advisory services, audits, reporting guidance, and simplified digital procedures—can reduce knowledge barriers and transaction costs and widen participation without lowering standards in terms of monitoring and achievement of sustainability objectives.
- **Reinforcing and mainstreaming sustainability considerations in the SME financing ecosystem**: Successful interventions not only finance individual projects but also embed sustainable lending practices more broadly in SME finance. This includes building the capacity of financial institutions to assess and manage green and sustainable investments, developing common standards and taxonomies, and promoting data-sharing systems that improve transparency. It also means supporting the emergence and growth of sustainability service providers that can offer relevant non-financial support for SMEs. By reinforcing the wider ecosystem, programmes can create demonstration effects, crowd in additional private capital, and ensure that sustainable finance for SMEs becomes mainstream.

Applying these lessons in practice can help countries adopt and scale solutions that are tailored to local contexts and responsive to the specific needs of SMEs. The OECD Committee on SMEs and Entrepreneurship, and its Platform on Financing SMEs for Sustainability, will continue their efforts to

1 Introduction

This chapter highlights the crucial role that SMEs play in the green transition. It examines key barriers such as limited financing access, and technical knowledge and capacity constraints. Emphasising the need for targeted interventions, the chapter underscores the importance of both public financial and non-financial support to help SMEs invest in and benefit from sustainable practice. It introduces the framework adopted in this report which segments SMEs into three categories, according to the role that they play in the green transition, namely SME innovators, enablers and adopters. Each of these actors requires distinct support mechanisms to drive innovation, scale sustainable solutions and adopt sustainable practices.

1.1. SMEs have a key role to play in the global sustainability agenda

Small and medium-sized enterprises (SMEs) are the backbone of economies worldwide, accounting for over 50% of business employment and economic output, and driving innovation and the provision of solutions to global challenges. Their role in advancing towards sustainability cannot be overlooked, as they collectively account for a substantial share of industrial pollution, waste, and resource consumption. According to recent OECD estimates, SMEs account for about 40% of business sector GHG emissions in EU countries, and about 50% globally according to the International Trade Centre (ITC) (OECD, 2023[1]; ITC, 2021[2]). SMEs also have an important role to play in devising the solutions to environmental challenges, accounting for 95% of the enterprises in cleantech-related manufacturing sectors across Europe (OECD, 2025[3]). Against the backdrop of intensifying climate change and increasing resource scarcity, greening SMEs is not just desirable but critical for achieving global sustainability goals.

SMEs, however, face considerable resource constraints when it comes to greening. In a 2023 global survey, 58% of SMEs identified skills and 44% lack of time as key barriers to climate action (SME Climate Hub, 2023[4]) The business case for green investments by SMEs is often constrained by high upfront costs and extended payback periods, which can strain the liquidity of small businesses and increase financial risk (Alliance for Financial Inclusion, 2024[5]). Uncertainties around evolving green technologies, fluctuating market demand for sustainable products, and shifting policies and regulations further increase investment risks. Administrative and regulatory burdens are an additional barrier. In the 2024 Eurobarometer survey on "SMEs, resource efficiency and green markets", EU SMEs identified the complexity of administrative or legal procedures (35%) and environmental reporting requirements (26%) among their main challenges (European Commission, 2024[6]).

Access to finance remains a critical challenge for SME greening. In a 2025 global survey of SMEs, 41% identified insufficient funding among the key barriers to climate action, and 63% reported having limited knowledge of available funding options for climate-related initiatives (SME Climate Hub, 2025[7]). According to the 2024 Eurobarometer survey, among the SMEs who have not yet undertaken any resource efficiency actions, nearly a quarter indicated that additional financial support would enable them to take such actions (European Commission, 2024[6]).

Most SMEs continue to rely on their own financial resources to implement resource efficiency measures. Only 35% of their sustainable investments are funded through external sources (European Comission, 2024[8]). Medium-sized enterprises are more likely than micro-enterprises to access both financial support (46% vs. 35%) and non-financial support (30% vs. 26%) from public institutions. The majority of SMEs still sees decarbonisation and investments in sustainability as synonymous with short-term risks and competitive disadvantages (Bpifrance, 2023[9]).

Limited access to financing is especially pronounced among SMEs in emerging markets and developing countries (EMDEs), where SMEs face additional barriers due to widespread informality, lacking credit history and collateral, as well as limited financial literacy regarding financing requirements. This in turn makes them more reliant on informal financial support from friends or family (Alliance for Financial Inclusion, 2024[5]). An IFC study identified formal SMEs in developing countries as having annual unmet financing needs of USD 5.2 trillion (International Finance Corporation, 2017[10]). A UNEP study showed that on average, 80% of loans distributed by banks in EMDEs required collateral, with collateral values reaching around 210% of the loan's value (United Nations Environment Programme, 2022[11]).

Additionally, green financing options offered by public financial institutions in EMDEs remain limited. For instance, only 20% of African banking portfolios are estimated to be green (European Investment Bank, 2020[12]). The lack of sustainable taxonomies and standardisation represents a further hurdle, creating challenges for comparability and reliability, raising transaction costs and increasing the risk of standardisation and green taxonomy as the main barrier in scaling up climate financing (Dalhuijsen et al., 2023[13]).

The lack of granular sustainability-related data from SMEs further exacerbates these challenges. It makes it difficult for SMEs to make informed decisions and for financial institutions to assess investment viability (Carvajal and Didier, 2024[14]). An OECD survey conducted in 2023 found that 60% of financial institutions are already requesting sustainability-related data from their SME clients, but these requests lack standardisation, ranging from informal questionnaires to externally validated assessments (OECD, 2023[15]).

1.2. Financial and non-financial support are critical for accelerating SME greening

Public financial support is critical to enable SMEs to gain access to a growing global pool of tailored financing solutions that integrate climate and other greening considerations in financing decisions and thereby offer more favourable financing conditions for clients with stronger sustainability credentials. In a 2023 OECD survey of public development banks and private financial institutions (FIs), the majority of respondents stated that they are integrating climate considerations in their operations, including in developing institutional objectives and plans (68%), assessing some or all financing/investment opportunities (66%) and providing dedicated financing programmes or more advantageous conditions for financing and investments focused on green objectives (72%). In the same survey, financial institutions noted that they are providing tailored financing solutions for SMEs' investments in net zero and greening, including through medium- and long-term loans (69%), short-term loans and factoring (38%), credit guarantees (67% of public development banks), and other financial instruments (OECD, 2023[15]).

Non-financial support also plays a critical role in enabling SMEs to transition toward greener practices. Capacity-building programmes, technical assistance, and advisory services can help equip SMEs with the necessary skills and information to make informed decisions about greening their operations. Additionally, these initiatives raise awareness about the economic and environmental benefits of sustainability supporting innovation and long-term investment and planning. Regulatory support, such as simplifying compliance procedures or offering clear guidance on environmental standards is also critical. All of this non-financial support also facilitates the provision of sustainable financing solutions for SMEs by financing providers.

Non-financial support can also help SMEs build the capacity to measure and report on their sustainability performance—a critical requirement for accessing green and sustainable finance. SMEs often lack the expertise or resources to meet reporting demands coming from their financing providers and supply chain partners. Conversely, financial institutions tend to structure their sustainability reporting requirements around large firms, making it difficult for SMEs to comply. Through training programmes, workshops, and targeted advisory services, non-financial support can enable SMEs to understand the benefits of adopting relevant reporting standards. Furthermore, tools and platforms provided by public or private initiatives can simplify data collection and reporting processes, reducing the burden on resource-constrained SMEs (OECD, 2024[16]).

1.3. Financial and non-financial support needs to be tailored to SMEs' diverse needs and contributions to the green economy

SMEs encompass a very wide range of enterprises, from microenterprises in local communities to highly specialised firms that are part of complex supply chains with global reach. With high diversity in terms of size, sector, geographic location and levels of technological maturity, SMEs play different roles in the greening of the economy, and they have diverse support needs, both in terms of financing as well as capacity building support. For the purposes of the analysis in this report, SMEs are considered in three broad categories:

- **Innovators** are SMEs and innovative start-ups that develop disruptive technologies and solutions to address the climate crisis and other environmental challenges. These pioneering companies are at the forefront of green innovation, creating new methods for carbon capture, sustainable energy storage, and advanced materials with minimal environmental impact. Their solutions facilitate the transformation of business operations toward green and sustainable practices. They need financial support to address key challenges such as high upfront costs, technical risks and market barriers. As such, they need more patient capital, such as R&D grants, equity and quasi-equity funding to support research, development, and commercialisation of their products and services (Note: for definitions of specific instruments please refer to the Glossary). When it comes to non-financial support, SME innovators can benefit especially from access to research, collaboration opportunities with universities and R&D institutions, and streamlined regulatory approval processes for green technologies. They can also benefit from mentorship programs, innovation hubs, and exposure to potential clients and markets to scale their solutions.
- **Enablers** are SMEs and start-ups that help disseminate green products and solutions and thereby enable their wider adoption among SMEs as well as large enterprises. Their facilitation of decarbonisation within supply chains and across ecosystems amplifies the impact of sustainability efforts far beyond their own operations. Enablers include renewable energy producers, installers, and providers or repair and maintenance services; recycling and waste management companies; green engineering and consultancy services providers; and others. Enablers can benefit from publicly provided financing solutions that support the scale-up and diversification of their operations, such as sector-specific loan and grant programmes, as well as risk-sharing mechanisms, such as guarantees, blended finance, and concessional funding. Trade finance solutions that facilitate enablers' exports and supply chain integration are also critical to help these businesses to grow their operations and gain market access. Enablers further need technical and capacity building support, such as support with standardisation, certifications and reporting. They can also benefit from access to collaborative ecosystems, such as industry networks and business forums, to help them deliver effective solutions and reach new customers. Finally, policies that promote partnerships between enablers and adopters can help enablers expand their market reach.
- **Adopters** account for the vast majority of SMEs globally, spanning most product and service sectors. They need to adopt green technologies and processes to decarbonise or otherwise improve the sustainability of their operations. As a result, these actors often require accessible and affordable financing options such as grants, leases, low-interest loans or sustainability-linked financing to overcome upfront investment costs. They can further benefit from financing solutions that de-risk green investments both for SMEs as well as financing providers, such as guarantees and blended finance solutions. SME adopters also need information and awareness support to understand the benefits, costs, and regulatory requirements of sustainable practices, facilitated by access to information portals with regulatory and policy updates, market insights and case studies demonstrating successful transitions. They also often require technical support to identify, integrate, and maintain green solutions such as energy efficiency upgrades, renewable energy systems, and circular economy strategies. Finally, capacity-building support is essential for securing green finance, ensuring regulatory compliance, optimising supply chains, and training staff, enabling SMEs to enhance competitiveness while also meeting their sustainability goals.

Table 1.1. SMEs need different support based on their roles in the green transition

	Definition	Relevant financial support	Relevant non-financial support
Innovators	SMEs that develop breakthrough technologies and green solutions.	Patient capital, including R&D grants, equity, and quasi-equity funding, to support the development, research, and commercialisation of innovative green solutions.	Access to research, collaboration opportunities, streamlined regulatory processes, mentorship programmes, innovation hubs, and global market exposure to scale solutions.
Enablers	SMEs that provide products and services that help other businesses, including larger corporations, decarbonise and improve the sustainability of their operations.	Debt, grants, risk-sharing mechanisms and trade finance solutions to help scale operations and facilitate market access and supply chain integration.	Technical assistance, capacity building, standardisation, certifications, and access to industry networks to enhance operations and expand market reach.
Adopters	SMEs that adopt green technologies and processes to improve the sustainability of their operations.	Direct and indirect financing instruments which lower high upfront costs and de-risk green investments.	Educational and awareness raising services on the benefits of greening, as well as technical and capacity-building support on implementation and enhancing competitiveness.

This report examines effective public financial and non-financial support practices that help SMEs contribute to the green transition. It analyses a range of financial instruments, such as green loans, grants, equity financing, and guarantees, and complementary measures like capacity-building and technical assistance. Drawing on case studies, the report highlights successful and innovative programmes, synthesising key lessons to guide policymakers, development banks, and SME agencies in designing and scaling effective interventions that drive SME innovation, enable green activities, and reduce environmental impacts.

The report is organised in four chapters. Chapters 2 through 4 are structured around the three SME profiles - innovators, enablers, and adopters - examining both financial and non-financial support available to each subset of SMEs. Chapter 5 provides a summary of lessons learned from implementation of greening-related financing and non-financial support to SMEs, including key challenges and success factors, drawing on desk research as well as case studies. Annex A at the end of the report contains 21 case studies.

1.4. References

Alliance for Financial Inclusion (2024), *Green Transition Measures for MSMEs*. [5]

Bpifrance (2023), *Trésorerie, investissement et croissance des PME/TPE*, https://lelab.bpifrance.fr/enquetes/la-tresorerie-des-tpe-et-pme-s-ameliore-et-les-marges-resistent-au-printemps-2023. [9]

Carvajal, A. and T. Didier (2024), *Financing Mitigation and Adaptation to Climate Change for SMEs (forthcoming)*. [14]

Dalhuijsen, E. et al. (2023), *Greening National Development Financial Institutions. Trends, Lessons Learned, and Ways Forward.*. [13]

European Comission (2024), *Market practices compendium for sustainable finance: Report of the Platform on Sustainable Finance*. [8]

European Commission (2024), *Eurobarometer survey 2024: SMEs, resource efficiency and green markets*, https://europa.eu/eurobarometer/surveys/detail/3221. [6]

European Investment Bank (2020), *Banking in Africa: financing transformation amid uncertainty.* [12]

International Finance Corporation (2017), *MSME Finance Gap. Assessment of the Shortfalls and Opportunities in Financing Micro, Small and Medium Enterprises in Emerging Markets.* [10]

ITC (2021), *SME Competitivness Outlook 2021: Empowering the Green Recovery.* [2]

OECD (2025), *Powering the future: the evolution of cleantech manufacturing and implications for FDI and SME linkages across Europe*, https://www.oecd.org/en/publications/the-evolution-of-cleantech-manufacturing_be87b21b-en.html. [3]

OECD (2024), *Fostering convergence in SME sustainability reporting: A background study.* [16]

OECD (2023), *Assessing greenhouse gas emissions and energy consumption in SMEs: Towards a pilot dashboard of SME greening and green entrepreneurship indicators*, https://www.oecd-ilibrary.org/environment/assessing-greenhouse-gas-emissions-and-energy-consumption-in-smes_ac8e6450-en;jsessionid=hXk9cJQk0B7u_-cYU4fFqBkgn3uQrThkXphqB2ee.ip-10-240-5-34. [1]

OECD (2023), *Financing SMEs for sustainability – Financial institution strategies and approaches: Results of an OECD survey of public and private financial institutions, OECD SME and Entrepreneurship Papers, No. 46*, https://doi.org/10.1787/b3fe3647-en. [15]

SME Climate Hub (2025), *SME Climate Hub Small Business 2025 Survey*, https://smeclimatehub.org/the-sme-climate-hub-survey/. [7]

SME Climate Hub (2023), *Small Business Climate Action, 2023 Survey*, https://smeclimatehub.org/sme-climate-hub-survey-2023/. [4]

United Nations Environment Programme (2022), *Assessing Green Financing Mechanisms for Micro, Small and Medium Enterprises (MSMEs) in Africa.* [11]

2 SME innovators: Financial and non-financial support mechanisms

This chapter examines the financial and non-financial support requirements of SME innovators that are driving the green transition. Drawing on a range of financing instruments such as R&D grants, concessional loans, blended finance, equity and quasi-equity mechanisms and innovation support programmes, it provides a comprehensive overview of how public institutions across OECD countries and beyond are adapting their financial support policies to meet the specific needs of green SMEs and start-ups. The chapter also showcases how non-financial measures such as mentorship through incubators and accelerators, advisory and technical assistance services, and access to collaborative innovation networks help to strengthen SMEs' capacity to develop, test and commercialise sustainable technologies.

Innovative small business face significant opportunities but also challenges in the green transition. On the one hand, they are uniquely positioned to capitalise on the growing demand for sustainable solutions, as both consumers and governments increasingly prioritise environmental responsibility. Innovators can also take advantage of the changing regulatory and policy requirements which demand greater transparency with respect to environmental performance, both within businesses' own operations and across their supply chains. On the other hand, green innovators face challenges related to limited access to funding, high research and development costs, long product development timelines, and navigating complex regulatory requirements. Due to their small size, they further face difficulties in scaling their innovations because of limited resources, competition from larger firms, and uncertain market demand, including, in some cases, the need to develop a specific product market and build consumer awareness.

Access to finance is an important challenge for SME green innovators. Developing and commercialising new green technologies involves significant risks, including uncertainties about technological feasibility, market acceptance, and regulatory approval, extensive research and development (R&D) and prototype testing before market readiness, and high upfront costs that private investors are often reluctant to bear alone (Owen and Vedanthachari, 2023[1]), (Harrer and Owen, 2022[2]), (Mukherjee et al., 2024[3]). Additionally, many green innovation projects are built around intangible assets, such as intellectual property, which are harder to evaluate and use as collateral, making them less attractive for traditional loans (Mina et al., 2021[4]). As a result, equity and quasi-equity financing, which allow for risk and reward sharing, are often better suited for these innovators. However, accessing equity financing presents its own challenges, as climate-related innovation receives a disproportionately low share of private capital, accounting for only 5.4% of total private market investments between 2017 and 2021 (Carvajal and Didier, 2024[5]).

Venture capital (VC) remains a limited source of finance for early-stage green innovation. While VC investment in climate tech has grown, most funds continue to prioritise projects with shorter-term commercial potential, leaving high-risk, capital-intensive climate technologies underfunded (Mašek and Plaček, 2024[6]). Persistent barriers include technological uncertainty, long development cycles, and regulatory risk, which reduce VC appetite for early-stage green ventures (Mukherjee et al., 2024[3]) (McKinsey, 2024[7]). Evidence from U.S. funding rounds suggests that environmental orientation ("green signals") improves VC outcomes at early and later stages, but has little effect at the seed stage where financing gaps are greatest (Hossnofsky et al., 2025[8]). Market analyses similarly show that early-stage climate tech remains resilient but relies heavily on complementary public finance and mission-driven capital to offset risks and attract private investment (SVB, 2025[9]).

To address these gaps, public financial support is crucial, both through direct funding, such as grants and equity and quasi-equity from publicly managed funds, and through incentives that encourage private venture capital and private equity firms to invest in green innovation. Additional mechanisms such as blended finance instruments, and targeted risk-sharing initiatives can also help lower costs for innovators and de-risk projects.

Non-financial support also has a key role to play in aiding SME innovators, as they often face challenges related to research, capacity building and market access. Providing SMEs with access to research facilities, as well as capacity building support through incubators and accelerators, which provide mentorship and advice, can be very helpful in addressing gaps innovators face in terms of knowledge and technical expertise. Such support can also help SMEs address challenges in navigating complex regulatory requirements and standards and facilitate market entry. Research support to SME innovators can further be provided through granting them access to testbeds, where SMEs can test their solutions in real-world environments. Additionally, green innovators often lack access to networks and market opportunities, making it difficult to connect with potential partners, customers, and investors who could support their growth. Therefore, support in the form of networking platforms, market facilitations and trainings and

2.1. Financial support for SME innovators

Key objectives of public financial support for SME innovators in the green transition include:

- **Early-stage research and development (R&D)**: Developing novel technologies often requires substantial upfront investment while facing significant technical and market uncertainty, amplified by information asymmetries about future commercial potential (Bergset, 2018[10]). A KfW study on SME innovators found that high costs (34%) and high risks (31%) were the main financial barriers, followed by limited internal (25%) and external (19%) financing. (Zimmermann, 2022[11]). Similar patterns are observed in green and deep-tech innovation, where long development cycles and technological risk hinder access to private capital (Mukherjee et al., 2024[3]). Venture capital and private equity generally favour projects with shorter-term commercial potential, limiting their involvement in experimental or pre-commercial R&D (Mašek and Plaček, 2024[6]; McKinsey, 2024[7]). Public financing mechanisms—such as grants, R&D tax credits, and blended finance—are thus critical to support experimentation, prototyping, and proof-of-concept work and to help crowd in private investment as technologies mature.
- **De-risking innovation**: SMEs and start-ups face persistent risk and uncertainty when moving from R&D to early commercialisation. At this stage, the commercial viability of their products remains unclear, and investors lack sufficient data to assess feasibility—a gap often described as the "Valley of Death" (Mukherjee et al., 2024[3]). Public institutions can help mitigate these risks through targeted mechanisms such as grants and equity participation, as well as blended finance structures and guarantees, which absorb a portion of the financial risk and encourage private capital to participate.
- **Market entry and scalability**: Bringing green solutions to market often requires significant additional investments to build supply chains, scale production, and establish distribution channels. Regulatory uncertainty adds to investor hesitation (Demirel and Parris, 2015[12]). Laws and regulations were identified as a key barrier by 32% of SME innovators (Zimmermann, 2022[11]). Public financing mechanisms such as commercialisation grants, venture capital or concessionary loans can help SMEs cover these costs and de-risk market entry.

Financing instruments that can help address the challenges of SME green innovators include R&D grants, concessional and blended finance, equity and quasi equity financing, incubators and accelerators and innovation prizes (Table 2.1):

Table 2.1. Common financial support instruments for SME green innovators

Financial support instrument	Description	Examples
R&D grants	Direct financing in the form of grants to support innovative research and development projects focused on environmental sustainability, aiming to accelerate the creation and adoption of green technologies	• R&D grants for upgrading energy systems • Financing for developing clean energy technologies
Concessional loans	Credit offered to SMEs and start-ups at favourable terms, such as reduced interest rates or extended repayment periods, to support their green projects	• Concessional loans for production of innovative green technologies
Blended finance	Strategic use of public or philanthropic capital to de-risk investments and attract private capital into projects that deliver environmental benefits	• Blended funding programmes for innovative sustainable projects
Equity and quasi equity finance	Capital for green businesses in exchange for ownership stakes (equity) or rights linked to financial performance, such as profit-sharing or convertible debt (quasi-equity), often designed to support innovative or high-risk green ventures or projects.	• Venture capital for development of green tech • Convertible or subordinated loans • Profit participation funding • Mezzanine financing
Incubators and accelerators	Programmes that provide mentorship, resources, and funding opportunities to early-stage start-ups that are developing innovative green initiatives	• Programmes offering seed funding for sustainability projects • Funding & networking opportunities for green tech start ups
Innovation prizes	Initiatives that offer financial rewards or other incentives to SMEs developing disruptive, green technologies	• Prizes for innovative clean energy solutions • Rewards for improvements in circularity

R&D grants provide non-dilutive funding (i.e. capital that does not require giving up equity or ownership of the business), allowing innovative companies to invest in high-risk, high-reward research without having to give up part of the ownership or operational control. R&D grants can help cover costs associated with experimentation, prototype development, and feasibility studies. Additionally, these grants can act as a signal to private investors, increasing confidence and attracting follow-on funding. Box 2.1 showcases examples of R&D grant instruments including Norway's grants for environmental technology innovation and implementation. Finland is also supporting SMEs who are developing innovative energy decarbonisation solutions which enhance grid flexibility (see case study in Annex A. Business Finland - Flexible Energy Systems programme).

Concessional finance enables green innovators to access affordable capital to develop, test, and scale innovative sustainable solutions. By offering preferential terms, public financial institutions help de-risk green innovation for SMEs and entrepreneurs and attract co-investment by private entities who may otherwise be reluctant to fund early-stage or experimental green technologies. Box 2.1 highlights examples of financial support, such as investment grants and interest rate subsidies available to German SMEs through the Environmental Innovation Programme. Additionally, the Global Innovation Lab for Climate Finance provides SMEs and start-ups in emerging and developing economies with access to over 78 innovative financing instruments such as blended finance facilities, guarantees, and risk management tools to support their innovative green ventures. In Malaysia, SMEs from the manufacturing and service sectors can access concessional loans for the development of innovative green technologies (see case study on High Tech and Green Facility from SME Bank Malaysia in Annex A).

Box 2.1. Examples of direct and indirect financing instruments for green innovators

R&D grants

Denmark: The Innovation Fund Denmark offered grant funding to SMEs and start-ups carrying out industrial research for the green transition under its **Missionbooster** programme. Eligible projects included CO2 capture and storage, green fuels, circular economy, and green agriculture. Funding ranged from DKK 1.5 million to 5 million (EUR 195 000 to 650 000), covering up to 70% of total eligible costs, including material and equipment expenses, employee salaries, and services from external knowledge providers.

Finland: The **Flexible Energy Systems Program** in Finland offers R&D grants and loans to SMEs and start-ups developing decarbonisation solutions for energy systems. The funding supports research and early-stage commercialisation efforts. Eligible projects areas cover electricity, heating, cooling, and fuels, and can include innovations such as electrifying heating systems or integrating clean fuels. The programme further fosters collaboration with research institutions, providing strategic guidance, and networking opportunities to enhance market prospects and access to further funding. The programme is envisioned to be implemented over six years from 2024 to 2030.

Norway: Innovation Norway provides R&D grants for SMEs focused on developing and implementing innovative environmental technologies through its **Environmental Technology scheme**. Eligible technologies include those which align with the EU's Sustainable Taxonomy. Target groups are suppliers who develop environmental technologies for sale. The funding aims to reduce the risk of the investment for SMEs and potential investors through the provision of grants. The grant covers all research and development activities, apart from feasibility studies, which must be completed by the SME prior to applying. Companies must demonstrate the environmental impact and scalability of their solutions using relevant metrics such as CO_2 reduction or energy efficiency improvements. In addition, the programme can partially cover demonstration costs and employee training, with grant coverage for small enterprises covering up to 70% of the costs.

Sweden: The **LIGHTer SME** programme from **Vinnova** provides support to SMEs who are developing innovative lightweight technology for Swedish industry. Key focus areas include optimisation of energy and resource efficiency, as well as circularity. The programme offers grants of up to SEK 500,000 (EUR 44 000) for small business projects, such as prototype development or demonstration of manufacturing techniques in collaboration with relevant partners. Deep tech projects, which includes research-intensive start-ups and SMEs are also eligible, and can receive can grant funding of up to SEK 750 000 (EUR 66 000). Priority is given to SMEs who have not previously received public research funding. All projects require co-financing to be eligible. Total programme budget amounts to SEK 6 million (EUR 528 000), and projects can be supported over a three-to-12-month timeline.

EU: The **European Commission** has raised EUR 93.5 billion for the 2021 to 2027 period for its **Horizon Europe** project to fund research and innovation through grants and equity investments. One of the key clusters which SMEs can access is *climate change, energy and mobility*. To access funding, SMEs must show how their projects align with the EU green priorities, their innovative potential, environmental impact and ability to scale. The first phase supports technical and commercial feasibility with grants of up to EUR 50 000, with a 70% co-financing rate. The second phase supports project development and demonstration, with grants of up to EUR 2.5 million. The **EIC Accelerator**, one of the subprogrammes, specifically targets SMEs and start-ups with innovative solutions, providing funding from the demonstration to market launch stage. SMEs can access a combination of grants and equity investments for their projects, with grants being earmarked for innovation activities, providing a 70% subsidy rate, whilst equity investments (ranging from EUR 500 000 to EUR 10 million) are intended to cover market deployment and scale up. The programme also provides SMEs with relevant non-financial support such as opportunities to engage in collaborative projects within the broader sustainability ecosystem.

Concessional finance

Germany: In Germany, SMEs are encouraged to participate in the **Environmental Innovation Programme**, offered by the public development bank **KfW** in collaboration with the **Federal Ministry for the Environment, Nature Conservation, Nuclear Safety and Consumer Protection**. The programme supports demonstration projects which reduce environmental impact in an innovative way, covering initiatives on circular economy, resource efficiency, and waste and water management, amongst others. Funding can be provided in two forms: investment grants of up to 30% or an interest rate subsidy to provide favourable financing conditions on KfW loans.

In **Malaysia,** the **SME Bank's High Tech & Green Facility** Programme offers concessional loans to innovative SMEs and start-ups in the manufacturing and services sectors, as well as start-ups who are developing innovative green technologies. Loans of up to RM10 million (EUR 2 million) are available to SMEs through participating banks for a term of up to 10 years, covering 80% of CAPEX and 100% of working capital costs. The programme offers a 3.5% profit rate (for loans without a guarantee) or 5% (for loans with a provided guarantee). Flexibility is available for repayment challenges, with options for rescheduling and restructuring.

In **Norway,** SMEs can gain access to concessional financing through the **Green Industry Financing Fund** from **Innovation Norway.** The fund supports activities critical to the net-zero transition, including the production of clean energy technologies such as batteries, solar panels, and wind turbines, as well as the manufacturing of key inputs, including critical raw materials. To be eligible, SMEs must be registered in Norway. Loans are offered below market-rates with the potential for interest free periods and extended grace periods. The total budget of the Fund amounts to NOK 5 billion (EUR 438 million).

Loan guarantees

Switzerland: The **Federal Office for the Environment (FOEN)** in Switzerland provides loan guarantees to SMEs and start-ups developing innovative green solutions through its **Technology Fund**. The primary aim of the fund is to de-risk lending for cleantech SMEs working on projects that contribute to reducing CO_2 emissions, enhancing energy efficiency, utilising renewable energy sources, and promoting the efficient use of resources. This support enables businesses to secure financing more easily from banks or other financial institutions. The loan guarantee can cover up to 100% of the loan amount, with a maximum coverage of CHF 3 million (EUR 3.2 million) and the loan term can extend up to 10 years. By providing these guarantees, the Technology Fund bridges the financing gap between equity funding in a start-up's early stages and standard corporate loans, enabling cleantech SMEs to access markets and scale their solutions.

Blended finance programmes

The **Global Innovation Lab for Climate Finance** is a public-private collaboration which supports entrepreneurs, start-ups and SMEs developing innovative solutions to address climate change challenges in emerging and developing countries. Since its creation in 2014, the Lab has launched over 78 innovative financing instruments. The instruments adopt a blended finance approach, utilising public or concessional financing to de-risk and attract private capital. Examples include the **Climate Resilience and Adaptation Finance and Technology Transfer Facility (CRAFT),** blending commercial and concessional capital into a private equity fund, as well as the Conexus Impact Fund, combining loans and guarantees with technical assistance. Call for ideas are launched, from which the most innovative and impactful projects are selected for funding. Participating entities can further benefit from networking opportunities and mentorship programmes. Funders include over 100 institutions from the public, private and philanthropic sector.

EU: The European Investment Bank (EIB) offered financing to SMEs developing innovative first-of-a-kind demonstration projects at the pre-commercial stage that contribute to the energy transition through its recently ended **InnovFin Energy Demonstration Projects programme**. The financing, ranging from EUR 7.5 million to 75 million, is available in the form of loans, loan guarantees, equity, or quasi-equity instruments, with a tenor of up to 15 years. Eligible projects include those that demonstrate commercial viability, enhance the competitiveness of manufacturing processes, and contribute to the energy transition. These include projects related to renewable energy technologies, flexible energy systems, energy storage, and carbon capture, utilization, and storage. The programme timeline spanned over six years from 2014 to 2020.

Sources: (Business Finland, 2025[13]), (European Commission, 2025[14]), (Innovation Norway, 2025[15]), (Innovation Fund Denmark, 2025[16]), (SME Bank, 2025[17]), (Climate Finance Lab, 2025[18]), (Bundesministerium für Umwelt, Naturschutz, nukleare Sicherheit und Verbraucherschutz (BMUV), 2025[19]), (EFTA Surveillance Authority, 2024[20]), (Federal Office for the Environment, 2025[21]), (European Investment Bank, 2025[22]), (Vinnova, 2023[23]).

Equity and quasi-equity financing: Publicly provided equity (e.g. venture capital) and quasi-equity instruments (e.g. subordinated debt, convertible debt, mezzanine financing, profit participation, etc.) enable investments in high-risk green ventures that would not otherwise be financed by private actors. The focus on green innovation and start-ups in particular creates additional considerations and requirements for public support. For instance, since many green ventures, such as renewable energy, circular economy models, or cleantech start-ups, have longer development cycles, public support mechanisms must accommodate longer time horizons than typical VC investments. Furthermore, since green investments often require demonstration of not only financial returns but also sustainability impact, these financing programmes may also require the development of impact assessment frameworks with sustainability-related key performance indicators (e.g. avoided emissions, resource efficiency, etc.). Market barriers, such as insufficient demand for sustainable products may also pose challenges for scaling and growth of these ventures and thus public support may need to include additional funding or complementary policy support for market development.

Examples of various equity and quasi equity financing solutions that have been deployed to support SME green innovators are included in Box 2.2. In the Netherlands, for example, Invest-NL supports innovative green start-ups through equity and subordinated loans, complemented by non-financial advisory and networking services to help scale and commercialise their technologies. In India, innovative start-ups can access equity funding with complementary non-financial support services from the Neev II Fund (see case study from SBTI Ventures in India Annex A). In Canada climate technology firms can access late-stage seed to growth-stage capital through the Climate Tech Fund II (see case study from the BDC in Annex A; (OECD, 2025[24])). Early-stage companies can access seed capital funding through Asian Development Bank (ADB) Ventures (see case study on ADB Ventures in Annex A).

Box 2.2. Examples of equity and quasi equity financing for green innovators

Canada: The **Climate Tech Fund II (CTF II),** launched by the **Business Development Bank of Canada (BDC)** in November 2022, is a CAD 400 million initiative aimed at investing in Canadian climate technology firms with high potential to become global leaders and significantly reduce greenhouse gas emissions. This fund builds upon BDC's initial CAD 600 million Cleantech Practice, bringing its total commitment in the cleantech and climate tech sectors to CAD 1 billion. CTF II focuses on providing late-stage seed to growth-stage capital to companies developing impactful technologies across various themes, including energy, mobility, built environment, industry and resources, and carbon management.

Estonia: Greentech start-ups in Estonia can benefit from the **SmartCap Green Fund**. Investments from this fund can range from EUR 500 000 to EUR 5 million and can go from seed funding up to expansion stage funding. The fund has raised a total of EUR 100 million. Innovative solutions should be related to climate change mitigation and adaption, sustainable water use, circular economy, pollution prevention, or biodiversity and ecosystem restoration measures. The fund is partially funded by NextGenerationEU recovery funds.

France: The French public development bank **Bpifrance** is supporting SMEs from the Technology, Environment, and Energy (TEE) sector who are specialising in renewable energies, the circular economy, energy efficiency and environmental services. Through the **France Energy and Environment Investment Fund 2 (FIEE 2),** a buyout fund, which has a target size of EUR 240 million, Bpifrance provides funding ranging from EUR 0.5 million to EUR 20 million. This financial support aims to accelerate the development and growth of TEE companies.

India: The **Neev II Fund** is operated by **SBICAP Ventures Limited**, a subsidiary of the **State Bank of India (SBI)** with additional funding from **EIB**. Launched in 2021, the fund provides equity and quasi-equity capital to SMEs in India that are working on innovative solutions in areas such as clean energy, electric vehicles, resource efficiency, water management, and circular economy. The fund targets SMEs offering products or services with significant ESG benefits. The fund has raised a total of EUR 125 million, to which the EIB has contributed EUR 25 million.

India: The **Green India Venture Fund (GIVF)** is a domestic venture capital fund managed by **IFCI Venture Capital Funds Limited**, established to invest in companies implementing Clean Development Mechanism (CDM) projects and other commercially viable ventures within India. With a corpus of INR 220 crore (USD 26.5 million and EUR 24.4 million), raised from domestic banks, financial institutions, insurance companies, and high-net-worth individuals, GIVF targets sectors such as energy, energy storage, waste management, pollution control, and manufacturing. The fund typically invests between INR4.5 crore (USD 540 000 EUR 0.5 million) and INR30 crore (USD 3.6 million and EUR 3.3 million) in early-stage and growth-stage companies, aiming for a target return of 20% per annum.

Italy: Cassa Depositi e Prestiti (CDP) is supporting SME innovators through its **Green Transition Fund** with a total amount of EUR 250 million. The fund targets SMEs and start-ups who are launching innovative green technology projects, covering areas such as renewable energy use, circular economy and energy efficiency measures, amongst others. The fund is partially funded through the NextGeneration EU Initiative. Objectives include improving access to finance for innovative SMEs and start-ups, as well as mobilising private sector investment into them. The fund provides both direct investments—including equity and quasi-equity —and indirect investments through third-party funds.

Netherlands: Invest-NL offers impact financing options to Dutch SMEs and start-ups focused on developing green solutions and sustainable technologies. Key focus areas include carbon neutrality, circular economy, and sustainable agriculture. Financing options include direct equity and quasi equity technologies, as well as debt financing in the form of subordinated loans. Invest-NL typically invests up to 50% of the total venture capital, with investments ranging from EUR 5 million to EUR 50 million. To further support green SMEs, Invest-NL offers guarantees to de-risk lending from private banks and investors, enabling SMEs to secure the capital needed to scale their solutions. In collaboration with the EIF, innovative SMEs can also access equity financing from the **Dutch Future Fund II (DFF II),** which has EUR 400 million available in funding. Key areas eligible for financing include the energy transition, agri-tech and circular economy. In addition to financial support, Invest-NL provides non-financial services such as strategic guidance on scaling operations, navigating regulatory developments, and identifying market opportunities. The agency also fosters networking opportunities, connecting businesses with relevant partners and stakeholders from the ecosystem.

Sweden: The **Almi Invest GreenTech Fund** is a Swedish venture capital fund established to invest in early-stage start-ups that significantly reduce greenhouse gas emissions or improve local environments. With approximately EUR 120 million under management, the fund focuses on sectors such as renewable energy, energy efficiency, recycling systems, energy storage, electrification, and sustainable materials. Since its inception, the fund has invested in around 40 companies. The Fund is co-financed by the EU.

UK: The **Low Carbon Innovation Fund (LCIF)** is a public-backed venture capital fund with over GBP 100 million in funding to support SME innovators in the East of England who are developing environmentally beneficial technologies, products or services. Eligible businesses must demonstrate that their green technologies, products or services have measurable greenhouse gas emission reductions. The fund aims to crowd in private investments and receives funding from the **European Regional Development Fund (ERDF)**. It is managed by public institutions such as the **Ministry of Housing, Communities and Local Government, University of East Anglia, and Norfolk County Council**, amongst others. As of now, over 82 SME innovators have received funding, leading to the development of over 100 new products, services and technologies which have been brought to the market. Funded projects have led to over 10 000 tons of CO_2 emissions being saved annually.

Asia: ADB Ventures, the venture arm of the **Asian Development Bank**, supports SME innovators and start-ups who develop solutions in the domains of clean energy, circular economy and sustainable agriculture, among others. The programme provides financial support in the form of patient venture capital, as well as seed capital to very early-stage companies, to enable them to pilot new climate solutions. The programme provides accompanying non-financial support.

The **EIF and EIB** are providing EUR 200 million in equity financing to SME cleantech ventures through the **Cleantech Co-Investment Facility.** Eligible projects are innovative green technologies or business models which align with the EIF's criteria for Climate Action and Environmental Sustainability. The EIF will co-invest alongside fund managers with tickets ranging from EUR 5 million and EUR 15 million. The investment is specifically meant to target the "second equity gap", which innovators face when moving from the start-up stage into the growth phase.

Sub-Saharan Africa: The **E3 Low Carbon Economy Fund I** (E3LCEF) is a venture capital fund co-managed by **E3 Capital and Cygnum Capital**, established to invest in early-stage innovative low-carbon entrepreneurs across sub-Saharan Africa. In May 2023, the fund achieved its first close at USD 48.1 million, with backing from development finance institutions including, among others, the German promotional bank **KfW**, the **Dutch Entrepreneurial Bank (FMO)** and the Swedish development finance institution, **Swedfund**. The fund provides both equity and quasi-equity financing structures to SMEs. E3LCEF focuses on early-stage companies offering low-carbon, decentralised, and smart services, aiming to support at least 16 start-ups specialising in renewable energies and related services such as e-mobility, connectivity, and energy efficiency tools across sub-Saharan Africa.

International: The **Althelia Climate Fund (ACF),** launched in 2013 and managed by **Mirova Natural Capital,** is a pioneering impact investment fund dedicated to financing projects that reduce deforestation, mitigate climate change, protect biodiversity, and support sustainable livelihoods for rural communities. The financing mechanisms include debt financing but also quasi equity financing (subordinated loans, profit-sharing agreements). With a global investment scope, ACF focuses on regions including Africa, Latin America, and Asia, supporting sustainable land use and conservation of primary forests. The fund employs a blended finance approach, pooling resources from both public and private investors, and has secured commitments from entities such as the **European Investment Bank (EIB),** which contributed up to EUR 25 million.

Sources: (Swedfund, 2025[25]), (Mirova, 2021[26]), (Almi, 2025[27]), (Business Development Bank of Canda, 2025[28]), (SmartCap, 2025[29]), (Bpifrance, 2025[30]), (European Investment Bank, 2025[31]), (IFCI Venture Capital Funds, 2021[32]), (ADB Ventures, 2025[33]), (European Investment Fund, 2025[34]), (University of East Anglia, 2025[35]), (InvestNL, 2025[36]), (CDP Venture Capital, 2025[37])

Incubators and accelerators not only offer mentorship and resources (see also non-financial support section below) but also act as conduits to funding by connecting SMEs with investors, venture capitalists, and public funding opportunities. Many incubators and accelerators provide direct financial support through grants, seed funding, or equity investments to help start-ups cover early-stage costs such as prototype development or market entry. Additionally, they often partner with public institutions to deliver funding programs, leveraging government-backed grants or subsidies to de-risk innovation. By creating a network of investors, accelerators and incubators also improve SMEs' chances of securing follow-on funding from venture capital firms or angel investors. Furthermore, they assist SMEs in preparing for investor engagement, offering guidance on pitching, financial planning, and sustainability reporting to attract green financing.

Some examples of financial support provided through incubators and accelerators are included in Box 2.3. For instance, the Accelerate2030 programme has supported over 480 entrepreneurs, connecting them with impact investors to encourage sustainable growth. The Deeptech plan programme of Bpifrance supports start-ups through mentorship, resources and access to financial support.

Box 2.3. Examples of financial support for innovators delivered through incubators and accelerators

France: In 2019, the French public development bank **Bpifrance** launched its **Deeptech Plan,** with a budget of EUR 3 billion, aiming to create 500 deeptech start-ups, with a strong focus on Greentech innovations. The programme provides start-ups with mentorship, resources, and access to financial support, contributing to their growth and integration into industrial sectors.

Kenya: The **Kenya Climate Innovation Center (KCIC),** launched through the **World Bank's Climate Technology Programme**, is providing incubation and scale-up support to innovative climate-related start-ups and early-stage SMEs through its **GreenBiz Programme**. Running from 2021 to 2025, GreenBiz targets 300 businesses developing climate-related technologies and innovative business models in five key sectors: water, renewable energy and energy efficiency, agriculture, commercial forestry, and waste management. Support is provided through a range of services, including business advisory, mentorship, technical assistance, capacity building, and financing. The programme is supporting 300 climate-tech ventures. It is funded by the **Danish International Development Agency (DANIDA).**

International: Accelerate2030 is a programme supporting start-ups and entrepreneurs in developing and emerging countries with innovative solutions which advance the UN's Sustainable Development Goals. The accelerator programme connects entrepreneurs with impact investors to support sustainable investment growth, enabling entrepreneurs to scale their solutions. To date, this programme has supported over 480 entrepreneurs.

Sources: (Accelerate2030, 2025[38]), (Bpifrance, 2024[39]), (KCIC, 2025[40])

Innovation prizes and competitions can enable SMEs and start-ups to obtain financial rewards for their proposals of developing innovative green technologies. These prizes provide funding to SMEs for advancing their solutions without taking on debt or diluting ownership. Additionally, winning an innovation prize enhances visibility, opening up opportunities for market entry, networking, and obtaining further investments. Such competitions further foster potential partnerships and increase visibility among consumers. Examples of this type of support are included in Box 2.4. For instance, European SMEs and start-ups working on circularity, energy efficiency and renewable energy use can participate in the European innovation Procurement Awards.

Box 2.4. Examples of innovation prizes for green start-ups and innovators

France: SMEs and start-ups can participate in the **i-Nov innovation competition** from **Bpifrance**. This competition focuses on supporting innovative projects, with a key pillar in Energy, Resources, and Natural Environments. The program provides funding of EUR 1 million to EUR 5 million per project, with 60% covered by a subsidy and the remaining 40% from recoverable advances.

EU: The **European Commission** offers **European Innovation Procurement Awards**, particularly targeted at SMEs and start-ups. The *Net Zero Industry Procurement* category rewards innovative solutions which promote circularity, energy efficiency and the use of renewable energy in industry. Awards range from EUR 25 000 to EUR 75 000.

ClimateLaunchpad, co-funded by the **European Union**, is a green business idea competition for entrepreneurs. Projects covering areas such as renewable energy, sustainable food systems and mobility can participate. Selected participants will benefit from bootcamps and coaching sessions to build up an effective business plan, as well as networking opportunities. At the end of the programme, businesses have the chance to gain prizes of from EUR 2 500 up to EUR 10 000.

Sources: (Bpifrance, 2025[41]), (European Innovation Council, 2025[42])

2.2. Non-financial support for SME innovators

Non-financial support can assist SME green innovators by complementing financing instruments and it often serves as a catalyst for growth and innovation. This type of support includes mechanisms such as R&D facilitation through collaborative programmes, incubators and accelerators, as well as access to testbeds and pilot initiatives (Table 2.2). These support mechanisms help SMEs refine their technologies, validate business models, and connect with key stakeholders across the innovation ecosystem.

Table 2.2. Non-financial support programmes for SME innovators

Support programme	Description	Examples
Green R&D collaboration programmes	Matchmaking services and funding which enable SMEs to access research facilities and relevant research partners	• Cooperation networks and matchmaking services which facilitate partner matching • Access to government research facilities
Green incubator and accelerator programmes	Tailored support to facilitate growth and commercialization through mentoring and technical assistance services	• Training programmes on developing growth business models • Networking and matchmaking to relevant consumers and partners
Green testbed and pilot programmes	Real-world testing facilities to demonstrate and validate innovative technologies	• Physical facilities and services which enable testing of solutions • Matchmaking services with relevant partners

R&D collaboration programmes bring together SME green innovators, research institutions, universities, and industry players to co-develop breakthrough sustainable technologies and solutions. These programs create opportunities for SMEs to access advanced research facilities, expertise, and funding while benefiting from knowledge-sharing and innovation ecosystems. By pooling resources and expertise, SMEs can overcome the high costs and risks associated with early-stage innovation. Governments and public financial institutions often support these initiatives by providing grants, matching funds, or tax incentives for collaborative R&D.

Examples of greening-oriented R&D collaboration programmes are illustrated in Box 2.5. This includes the Innovative Solutions Canada Programme, which gives innovators access to R&D facilities, government expertise and networks. In Türkiye, innovative SMEs are supported through a 6-month programme which provides matchmaking services, business model development and commercialisation support.

Box 2.5. Examples of R&D collaboration programmes

Canada: The **Innovative Solutions Canada (ISC) Programme** offers support to SMEs and start-ups with innovative solutions through providing them with access to government expertise, facilities and networks. The centre facilitates connections between SMEs and relevant partners to prove feasibility, test and scale their solutions, as well as providing complementary funding. The programme further provides support on market entry. Key target areas of the programme include green technology solutions such as solar panel recycling or low carbon construction materials.

Türkiye: Türkiye's **Scientific and Technological Research Council (TÜBİTAK)** is offering support to SME innovators through the **Industrial Innovation Network Mechanism (SAYEM)** programme. This programme offers a platform aiming to encourage collaborations between innovators, universities and government agencies for innovative R&D projects which target sustainable growth. The programme operates in two phases: first, forming innovation networks with a business roadmap, and second, supporting product commercialisation with grants for R&D implementations. Projects are supported for one year, with each phase lasting six months. After this, a process can be launched which monitors the success of the commercialisation of the product, which can lead to a possible extension in support. This initiative aims to stimulate green industrial innovation through knowledge sharing and cross sectoral collaboration.

Incubator and accelerator programs provide tailored support to SME green innovators at different stages of their journey, from ideation to scaling. Incubators focus on early-stage start-ups, offering resources such as office space, mentoring, and technical assistance to refine ideas and prototypes. Accelerators, on the other hand, help SMEs scale their innovations through intensive business development, market access, and investor connections. These programmes often include funding opportunities, networking events, and training on topics such as commercialisation and sustainability metrics. For green innovators, incubators and accelerators designed around sustainability goals can provide critical resources and guidance to turn ideas into market-ready solutions, while aligning with environmental impact objectives.

Examples of green innovator support through incubators and accelerators are included in Box 2.6. In the EU, SMEs and entrepreneurs can benefit from tailored coaching services, access to resources and matchmaking services through the EIT Climate-KIC Accelerator. The Asian Development Bank (ADB) supports SMEs with piloting opportunities and market entry.

Box 2.6. Examples of incubator and accelerator support programmes

Finland: Business Finland provides market access advisory services and fosters international collaboration and networking opportunities for Finnish SMEs and start-ups developing innovative energy solutions. Support includes guidance on navigating international regulations, insights into global end-user needs, and matchmaking with suitable partners. Start-ups can access the 'Dealflow Finland'' portal, which connects them with impact investors.

Asia: The **ADB Venture Lab**, the technical assistance arm of the venture capital fund of the **Asian Development Bank**, provides support to innovative start-ups through connecting them with relevant partners. The programme accelerates market entry by fast-tracking solutions and facilitating piloting opportunities.

Europe: The **EIT Climate-KIC Accelerator**, funded by the **EU**, supports cleantech entrepreneurs by providing tailored coaching, educational services, and access to tools and resources. The programme helps start-ups develop business models, identify target customers, and connect with relevant partners and investors through matchmaking services. To date, it has supported over 150 start-ups.

International: The **Cleantech Innovation Programme**, a collaboration between the **Global Environmental Facility** and the **United Nations Industrial Development Organization,** supports SMEs and start-ups in low- and middle-income countries to scale innovative solutions that reduce greenhouse gas emissions and drive sustainable economic growth. It offers direct support to SMEs through customised accelerator programmes with tailored training and advisory services to help SMEs refine their business models, scale operations, and secure investment. Adopting an ecosystem approach, the programme connects SMEs with key public and private stakeholders while providing policy guidance to countries to strengthen regulatory frameworks for fostering innovation.

Caribbean: The **Eastern Caribbean Greenpreneurs** programme by the **Global Green Growth Institute (GGGI)** is a three-year programme which helps entrepreneurs and start-ups working on innovative green solutions. It offers capacity-building, mentorship, networking opportunities and funding support to help start-ups in the Caribbean region scale their sustainable businesses. The incubator programme targets MSMEs with demonstrated growth potential who are showcasing scalable green business models. High potential start-ups can be award them with repayable grants of up to USD 50 000, as well as facilitating links with potential investors.

Sources: (EIT Climate-KIC, 2025[45]), (Climate Launchpad, 2025[46]), (UNIDO, 2025[47]), (ADB, 2020[48]), (GGGI, 2025[49]) (Business Finland, 2025[50])

Test beds and pilot programmes provide SME green innovators with real-world environments to validate and demonstrate their sustainable technologies or solutions. These programmes reduce the risks of scaling by allowing SMEs to test their innovations in controlled or operational conditions. Public institutions often facilitate access to these test environments by offering infrastructure, regulatory guidance, and funding. Successful pilot programs help SMEs prove the efficacy of their solutions, attract investors, and secure early adopters, accelerating the transition from prototype to commercialisation.

Examples of testbeds and pilots are included in Box 2.7. European SMEs, for instance, can use the Open Innovation Test Bed to test bio-based solutions, as well as receiving complementary technical support, market insights and funding support. Singaporean start-ups and SMEs providing solutions in waste management can apply for a testbed programme offered by the National Environment Agency (see Box 2.7).

Knowledge-sharing platforms provide SMEs with access to expertise by facilitating connections with industry experts, mentors, and other like-minded SMEs and start-ups. These platforms also create opportunities for collaboration, enabling SMEs to share resources, knowledge, and best practices. Additionally, by offering market insights, these platforms help SMEs with market entry. For instance, Austrian start-ups can participate in the Greentech Valley platform to benefit from networking and collaboration opportunities, as well as technical expertise on market entry (see Box 2.7).

Box 2.7. Examples of testbeds, pilots and knowledge-sharing platforms for green innovators

Testbeds and pilots

Singapore: The **National Environment Agency** is enabling SMEs and start-ups to testbed or demonstrate their **Waste-to-Energy solutions**. The initiative focuses on energy recovery from waste, improving resource efficiency, and reducing environmental impact. Participants can pilot their solutions in a real-world environment, to help the development and commercialisation of their proposed solution. Applicants need to articulate their deployment and commercialisation plans.

Europe: INN-PRESSME, a public-private collaboration co-funded by the **European Union**, offers an **Open Innovation Test Bed** to European SMEs developing bio-based solutions in sectors like energy, transport, and consumer goods. This testbed provides SMEs with access to physical facilities and services needed to develop, test, and scale their innovations. In addition to technical support, it offers market insights, circular economy assessments, funding support, and product certification services to support SMEs.

Europe: The European Institute of Innovation and Technology (EIT) is offering the **EIT Community Testbeds** for innovative start-ups and SMEs to test their solutions in a real-world environment. This initiative also offers opportunities for collaboration with other industry players and emerging start-ups, fostering further innovation.

Knowledge-sharing platforms

Austria: The **Greentech Valley** was established by the cleantech cluster **ECO WORLD STYRIA** in 2005 in Austria through a public-private partnership. It receives financial support from the **regional government of Styria** and serves as a platform to connect green Austrian cleantech SMEs working on biomass, solar energy, waste management and water efficiency. Greentech Austria provides SMEs with networking opportunities, business development support, market access, and collaboration platforms to help them scale their green innovations. The platform also offers access to funding, technical expertise, and advisory services to help SMEs enhance their green products and services.

Additionally, Greentech Austria facilitates connections between SMEs, research institutions, and industry players to accelerate the growth of the green tech sector in Austria and internationally.

US: The National Renewable Energy Laboratory (NREL) facilitates knowledge sharing between clean tech start-ups through its **Innovation and Entrepreneurship Center**. The centre offers networking and collaboration opportunities, connecting innovative start-ups with investors and industry stakeholders. It further offers tools and data which enable start-ups to obtain market insights and learn about best practices.

Sources: (INN PRESSME, 2023[51]), (EIT, 2025[52]), (National Environment Agency, 2025[53]) (Green Tech Valley, 2025[54]), (NREL, 2025[55])

2.3. References

Accelerate2030 (2025), *Accelerate2030*, https://accelerate2030.net/. [38]

ADB (2020), *ADB Unveils Venture Platform to Invest in Impact Technology Startups*, https://www.adb.org/news/adb-unveils-venture-platform-invest-impact-technology-startups. [48]

ADB Ventures (2025), *Our investments*, https://ventures.adb.org/. [33]

Almi (2025), *Almi Invest GreenTech*, https://www.almi.se/riskkapital/vara-riskkapitalbolag/almi-invest-greentech/. [27]

Bergset, L. (2018), "Green start-up finance – where do particular challenges lie?", *International Journal of Entrepreneurial Behavior & Research*, Vol. 24/2, pp. 451-475. [10]

Bpifrance (2025), *Concours d'innovation i-Nov*, https://www.bpifrance.fr/catalogue-offres/concours-dinnovation-i-nov. [41]

Bpifrance (2025), *Fonds Impact Environnement*, https://www.bpifrance.fr/nos-solutions/investissement-expertise/fonds-impact-environnement. [30]

Bpifrance (2024), *5 ans après le lancement du Plan Deeptech, l'écosystème deeptech a reconfiguré le paysage de l'innovation en France*, https://presse.bpifrance.fr/5-ans-apres-le-lancement-du-plan-deeptech-lecosysteme-deeptech-a-reconfigure-le-paysage-de-linnovation-en-fran. [39]

Bundesministerium für Umwelt, Naturschutz, nukleare Sicherheit und Verbraucherschutz (BMUV) (2025), *Umweltinnovationsprogramm*, https://www.bmuv.de/programm/umweltinnovationsprogramm. [19]

Business Development Bank of Canda (2025), *Climate Tech Fund*, https://www.bdc.ca/en/bdc-capital/venture-capital/funds/climate-tech-fund. [28]

Business Finland (2025), *Dealflow from Finland*, https://www.businessfinland.com/how-we-can-help/investor-services/. [50]

Business Finland (2025), *Flexible Energy Systems*, https://www.businessfinland.fi/en/for-finnish-customers/services/programs/flexible-energy-systems-program. [13]

Carvajal, A. and T. Didier (2024), *Financing Mitigation and Adaptation to Climate Change for SMEs (forthcoming)*. [5]

CDP Venture Capital (2025), *Green Transition Fund*, https://www.cdpventurecapital.it/cdp-venture-capital/en/fondo_green_transition.page. [37]

Climate Finance Lab (2025), *How the Lab works*, https://www.climatefinancelab.org/. [18]

Climate Launchpad (2025), *Competition*, https://climatelaunchpad.org/competition/. [46]

Demirel, P. and S. Parris (2015), "Access to finance for innovators in the UK's environmental sector", *Technology Analysis & Strategic Management*, Vol. 27/7, pp. 782-808. [12]

EFTA Surveillance Authority (2024), *The Green Industry Financing Fund*, https://www.eftasurv.int/cms/sites/default/files/documents/gopro/College%20Decision%20111%2024%20COL%20-%20State%20aid%20-%20Norway%20-%20Green%20industry%20loan%20scheme.pdf. [20]

EIT (2025), *EIT Community Testbeds*, https://testbeds.eitcommunity.eu/. [52]

EIT Climate-KIC (2025), *Accelerator*, https://www.climate-kic.org/programmes/climate-entrepreneurship/accelerator/. [45]

European Commission (2025), *Horizon Europe*, https://research-and-innovation.ec.europa.eu/funding/funding-opportunities/funding-programmes-and-open-calls/horizon-europe_en. [14]

European Innovation Council (2025), *European Innovation Procurement Awards*, https://eic.ec.europa.eu/eic-prizes/european-innovation-procurement-awards_en. [42]

European Investment Bank (2025), *InnovFin, Energy Demo Projects*, https://www.eib.org/files/publications/thematic/innovfin_energy_demo_projects_en.pdf. [22]

European Investment Bank (2025), *NEEV II*, https://www.eib.org/en/projects/all/20190889. [31]

European Investment Fund (2025), *Climate & Infrastructure Funds*, https://engage.eif.org/investeu/climate-infrastructure-funds. [34]

Federal Office for the Environment (2025), *Technology Fund*, https://www.technologyfund.ch/. [21]

GGGI (2025), *Greenpreneurs*, https://gggi.org/global-program/greenpreneurs/. [49]

Government of Canada (2025), *Innovative Solutions Canada*, https://ised-isde.canada.ca/site/innovative-solutions-canada/en. [43]

Green Tech Valley (2025), *Green Tech Valley. From pioneers to global market leaders*, https://www.greentech.at/en/uber-das-valley/. [54]

Harrer, T. and R. Owen (2022), "Reducing early-stage Cleantech funding gaps: an exploration of the role of Environmental Performance Indicators", *International Journal of Entrepreneurial Behavior and Research*, Vol. 28/9, pp. 268-288. [2]

Hossnofsky, V. et al. (2025), "Green signals of new ventures: investigating the impact of environmental orientation on funding and the moderating role of lead venture capitalists" Small Bus Econon, https://doi.org/10.1007/s11187-02. [8]

IFCI Venture Capital Funds (2021), *Green India Venture Fund*, [32]

INN PRESSME (2023), *Test before investing: INN-PRESSME Open Innovation Test Bed services*, https://www.inn-pressme.eu/test-before-investing-inn-pressme-open-innovation-test-bed-services/. [51]

Innovation Fund Denmark (2025), *Missionbooster*, https://innovationsfonden.dk/en/p/missionbooster. [16]

Innovation Norway (2025), *Grants for Environmental Technology*, https://en.innovasjonnorge.no/article/grants-for-environmental-technology. [15]

InvestNL (2025), *Financiering*, https://www.invest-nl.nl/nl/onze-aanpak/financiering. [36]

KCIC (2025), *GreenBiz Programme*, https://www.kenyacic.org/greenbiz/#1623413570879-536c21ae-9a64. [40]

Mašek, J. and J. Plaček (2024), "Exploring the Role of Venture Capital in Advancing Green Innovation", https://actamont.fberg.tuke.sk/pdf/2024/n4/5masek.pdf. [6]

McKinsey (2024), "A different high-growth story: The unique challenges of climate tech", https://www.mckinsey.com/capabilities/strategy-and-corporate-finance/our-insights/a-different-high-growth-story-the-unique-challenges-of-climate-tech. [7]

Mina, A. et al. (2021), "Public funding of innovation: Exploring applications and allocations of the European SME Instrument", *Research Policy*, Vol. 50/1, pp. 1-12. [4]

Mirova (2021), *Althelia Climate Fund Impact Report 2021*, https://www.mirova.com/sites/default/files/2021-07/ACF1%20Report%202021.pdf. [26]

Mukherjee, A. et al. (2024), "Financing green innovation startups: a systematic literature review on early-stage SME funding", *Venture Capital*, pp. 1-27. [3]

National Environment Agency (2025), *Waste-to-Energy (WTE) Test-bedding and Demonstration Funding Initiative [Closed for Applications]*, https://www.nea.gov.sg/programmes-grants/grants-and-awards/research-innovation-and-enterprise-funding-initiatives/wte-testbed-demo-initiative. [53]

NREL (2025), *Innovation & Entrepreneurship Center*, https://www.nrel.gov/innovate/. [55]

OECD (2025), *Benchmarking government support for venture capital: A comparative analysis, OECD SME and Entrepreneurship Papers, No. 71, OECD Publishing, Paris.*, https://doi.org/10.1787/81e53985-en. [24]

Owen, R. and L. Vedanthachari (2023), "Exploring the Role of U.K. Government Policy in Developing the University Entrepreneurial Finance Ecosystem for Cleantech", *IEEE Transactions on Engineering Management*, Vol. 70/3. [1]

SmartCap (2025), *SmartCap Green Fund Direct Investment Programme*, https://smartcap.ee/gtip-202210/. [29]

SME Bank (2025), *High Tech & Green Facility (HTG)*, https://www.smebank.com.my/high-tech-green-facility-htg-. [17]

SVB (2025), "The Future of Climate Tech 2025", https://www.svb.com/trends-insights/reports/future-of-climate-tech/. [9]

Swedfund (2025), *E3 Low Carbon Economy Fund I*, https://www.swedfund.se/en/investments-and-projects/e3-low-carbon-economy-fund-i. [25]

TÜBİTAK (2025), *1704 - SAYEM- Industrial Innovation Networks*, https://tubitak.gov.tr/en/funds/sanayi/ulusal-destek-programlari/1704-sayem-industrial-innovation-networks. [44]

UNIDO (2025), *Global Cleantech Innovation Programme*, https://www.unido.org/GCIP. [47]

University of East Anglia (2025), *Low Carbon Innovation Fund*, https://innovationfunding.uea.ac.uk/low-carbon-innovation-fund/. [35]

Vinnova (2023), *LIGHTer small business 2023*, https://www.vinnova.se/en/calls-for-proposals/Strategic-innovation-programme-for-lightweight/lighter-small-business-2023/ (accessed on 2025). [23]

Zimmermann, D. (2022), "Types of SMEs in the innovation system: activities, constraints and successes", *KfW Research*, Vol. 394, pp. 1-12. [11]

3 SME enablers: Financial and non-financial support mechanisms

This chapter explores how public financial and non-financial support can help SME enablers, who are disseminating green technologies and services, to scale up their operations and participate more effectively in domestic and international green markets. Such support may take the form of targeted financial instruments, risk-sharing mechanisms and trade facilitation measures designed to alleviate capital constraints and de-risk investments in green innovation. Complementary non-financial interventions, including business development services and market access support, further enhance the ability of enablers to diffuse green technologies and expand into global value chains.

SMEs act as enablers of the green transition by providing critical products, services, and solutions that facilitate sustainability efforts across industries and communities. These businesses often serve as intermediaries, connecting adopters and innovators of green technologies. For instance, SMEs in renewable energy distribution, such as installers of solar panels or local providers of energy-efficient appliances, help scale green technology adoption. Similarly, waste management SMEs contribute by collecting, sorting, and processing recyclable materials, enabling circular economy practices. Agricultural SME retailers or producers can green agricultural practices through installing water-efficient irrigation systems or providing inputs such as organic fertilisers and bio-pesticides. SMEs in consulting or engineering support larger firms in transitioning to sustainable operations by offering expertise in carbon accounting, energy audits, or sustainable supply chain design. By enabling others to achieve sustainability goals, these SMEs play an essential role in the broader green ecosystem.

The transition presents a range of opportunities for SME enablers. Growing demand for green technologies and sustainable services, from both businesses and consumers, opens new markets. At the same time, evolving policy and regulatory frameworks are increasingly supportive of green investments, encouraging SMEs to adopt and scale sustainable practices and building demand for products and services offered by enablers. In addition, the transition requires significant development of infrastructure and support services, offering further market opportunities for these firms.

At the same time, SME enablers face various challenges. The high up-front costs associated with developing and installing green products and technologies can present a significant barrier (European Commission, 2016[1]). Additionally, scaling operations is challenging due to limited access to capital, slow market adoption, and competition from larger firms which have more resources, better financing options, and established market presence. SME enablers may also lack awareness of relevant support schemes that they could tap into and navigating complex regulatory requirements can be very resource consuming. In addition, uncertainty surrounding the evolution of regulations can raise the risk profile of SME enablers and make their long-term planning and investment more challenging.

Enablers, like many SMEs in general, often face challenges in accessing global value chains (GVCs) due to the need to meet stringent supplier requirements, including quality standards, access networks, or scale production to match demand. Nine out of ten SMEs sell their green technologies only in domestic markets (SWITCH2Green, 2025[2]). Traditionally, SMEs are less likely than larger firms to join business networks, restricting their collaboration opportunities (OECD, 2023[3]). Integrating into GVCs is further complicated by SMEs' limited internal resources, such as managerial skills, technology, and innovation assets, as well as external challenges like restricted access to trade finance and inadequate physical infrastructure. In EMDEs, two thirds of SME suppliers cited financial constraints as the primary obstacle to integrating into GVCs (Global Partnership for Financial Inclusion, 2017[4]). Many SME enablers also lack digital intensity, missing out on digitalisation benefits that could lower operational costs and facilitate international expansion (OECD, 2023[3]).

3.1. Financial support for SME enablers

Public financial support for enablers can serve several important purposes:

- **Reducing upfront costs and financing risks:** Risk-sharing mechanisms, such as guarantees, blended finance, and concessional funding, can mitigate upfront costs and financing risks by absorbing potential losses for private financing providers and enabling more favourable financing terms and expanded credit access for recipient SMEs who are disseminating greening solutions.
- **Scaling up operations:** Public financial support can also alleviate the financial burden of scaling-up and diversifying production and entering new markets, both of which are particularly important

- **Supply chain integration:** Financing instruments like grants, guarantees, or supply chain financing can also help enablers address barriers to supply chain integration or expansion by funding investments in quality improvements, certification processes, or capacity building, which can further be complemented with relevant non-financial support (see section on non-financial support below).

Table 3.1. Common financial support instruments for SME green transition enablers

Financial support instrument	Description	Examples
Direct financing instruments		
Sector specific green loans	Direct financing in the form of loans which offer preferential terms such as low interest rates and longer repayment terms for SMEs from specific sectors providing environmental services	• Credit to energy service providers installing renewable energy technologies • Credit to producers of renewable energy
Sector specific green grants	Direct payments offsetting the high upfront costs of SMEs developing and implementing green technologies	• Grants for companies that provide resource efficiency services • Funding for installation of clean energy systems
Green revenue-based loans	Direct green financing mechanisms where repayment terms are tied to revenues generated from green projects	• Credit to renewable energy producers where repayment is tied to revenues generated from sales
Risk sharing instruments		
Credit guarantee schemes	Risk-sharing mechanisms which provide financial guarantees to lenders, reducing the risk of loans for businesses producing green technologies. Green guarantees offer more favourable financing terms than other guarantee instruments	• Guarantees for SME renewable energy enablers who are producing renewable energy or installing relevant technologies and systems
Blended finance	Strategic use of public or philanthropic capital to de-risk investments and attract private capital into projects that deliver environmental benefits.	• Programmes which provide funding for SME generators and providers of renewable energy solutions
Market based instruments		
Mini bonds	Debt issued by SMEs to finance greening investments as well mini bonds issued by SMEs themselves. Differs from other bonds in terms of financing conditions and premia for green performance.	• Mini bonds issued by SME enablers to finance sustainable infrastructure projects
Trade instruments		
Targeted trade and supply chain financing	Financing that facilitates enablers' exports or participation in supply chains through mechanisms for easing cash flow challenges or de-risking transactions	• Export support for producers of green solutions including clean energy

Public financial support in this category is tailored to SMEs offering green products and services that help other businesses reduce their emissions or improve sustainability. Some relevant instruments in this category include:

Sector-specific loan or grant programmes targeting SMEs in industries such as energy efficiency, recycling and greening service providers, can help enablers access necessary funding to mitigate investment costs and scale up operations. They can be provided directly to SMEs by relevant public development banks or equivalent public institutions. They may also be provided indirectly via financial intermediaries, which can include other public financial institutions, commercial banks or others. Some examples included in Box 3.1 include, for instance, a German debt-financing scheme for SMEs who are generating renewable energy for the electricity grid, covering up to 100% of the investment costs (see Box 3.1). Similarly, Danish SMEs developing clean technologies can access grant funding through the Green Accelerator programme, which provides technical assistance and support services to help them scale and export their green solutions (see case study on the Green Accelerator programme in Annex A).

Revenue-based financing schemes can be very useful for enablers as they offer a flexible alternative to traditional loans, where repayments are tied to a percentage of revenue rather than fixed instalments. This model reduces the burden on cash flow, making it particularly suitable for small sustainable businesses with fluctuating incomes or small businesses that are bringing new products to the market that require the building up of a customer base. In Korea, a revenue-based financing programme is being implemented by the IBK to support solar power generating companies (see Box 3.1).

Market-based instruments, such as green mini bonds, enable SMEs to access capital markets and funding for their green projects. By leveraging market dynamics, these instruments allow SME enablers to enhance their visibility, attract private investment, and secure the necessary funding to scale their green solutions. Subject to less regulatory oversight, mini bonds are often more accessible to SMEs, but to reduce investment risk, they are often backed by public financial institutions through credit enhancements or guarantees. In Italy, for example, green mini bonds from small and medium-sized water utility companies were pooled with the backing of the EIB and CDP for risk mitigation, enabling these utility companies to green their infrastructure (see Box 3.1).

Box 3.1. Examples of direct and indirect financing instruments for enablers

Sector-specific loans

France: The French public development bank **Bpifrance** is offering financing to SMEs for developing **methanisation units** which will feed into the gas network. Funding is for low-value tangible and intangible assets, provided in the form of unsecured loans. The loan amount can range from EUR 100 000 to EUR 1 million and has a repayment period of 3 to 12 years.

Germany: The regional **L-Bank** provides financing to **SME renewable energy generators** who are feeding their generated energy into the electricity grid or directly selling it. Financed clean energy projects include solar PV projects, hydroelectric power and clean energy generated through wind power. 100% of the investment costs can be financed, with amounts ranging from EUR 5 million to EUR 10 million. Repayment terms are flexible, ranging from 6 to 30 years with grace periods of up to two years. The interest rates are reduced and fixed for up to 20 years. Borrowers can benefit from a 12-month fee-free period for disbursements, after which a 0.15% monthly fee applies to undisbursed amounts. Innovative domains such as Agri-Photovoltaics offer special repayment terms and interest rate reductions.

New Zealand: The **New Zealand Green Investment Finance bank** is offering debt financing to SMEs who are providing low carbon products, services, or technologies through its **Green Finance Accelerator Programme**. Lending goes up to NZD 5 million and can be provided in the form of working capital, with a two-year repayment period, or asset finance, with repayment of up to five years. Examples of SMEs who have benefitted from the programme include "Thundergrid", which supplies EV charging stations and managing charging networks.

Green synthetic securitisation

Germany: The **Landesbank Baden-Württemberg (LBBW)** backed by a guarantee from the **EIB group** is providing financing to SMEs engaged in **renewable energy projects**. In this green synthetic securitisation operation, the EIB group is providing a guarantee of EUR 175 million on a mezzanine tranche of the LBBW's portfolio. This operation enables the freeing up of additional capital for LBBW, of which EUR 350 million will be allocated to lending for clean power projects. The intermediated approach enables LBBW to reach smaller scale renewable energy projects, which otherwise would not have been possible to reach directly. Eligible projects include solar energy, wind power, biomass, geothermal and other energy efficient technologies. The programme is expected to generate 340MW of electricity from renewable sources.

Sector-specific grant and subsidy programmes

Denmark: The **Export and Investment Fund of Denmark (EIFO)** though the **Green Accelerator programme** supports SMEs in exporting their clean technologies related to areas such as renewable energy, energy efficiency, efficient resource use, and waste management. The programme provides grant funding of up to EUR 300,000 upon project completion. The programme raised DKK 85 million (EUR 11 million) and subsidises costs such as consultancy services, feasibility studies, market research, legal advice, ESG compliance analyses, enabling SMEs to scale green solutions abroad.

Finland: The **Investment Aid for Circular Economy** programme provides SMEs with funding for initiatives which improve circular economy models of other businesses. Eligible investments for funding include industrial construction projects, such as new circular economy technologies, and digital solutions or innovative production lines which improve waste recycling of other businesses. SMEs can get a maximum of 45% of additional investment costs covered, and the grant can go up to EUR 15 million.

India: The **Uttar Pradesh government** in India adopted the **mini-grid policy** in 2016, providing financial support to SME renewable energy generators who are speeding up electrification in rural areas. Supported mini grid projects are those which generate up to 500kW of electricity. SME developers can access capital grants which cover up to 30% of costs, with the government choosing the project location, customer tariff, and technical specifications. Developers must supply 8 hours of electricity for homes and 6 hours for businesses, with the option to sell excess power to other customers. The tariff is Rs. 60/month for 50W, Rs. 120/month for 100W, and for loads above 100W.

Revenue-based loans

Korea: The **Industrial Bank of Korea** offers the **Solar Power Facility Financing Loan** to SMEs who are in the solar power industry and contributing to the transition to a low carbon economy. This financing programme offers loans to SMEs which cover up to 80% of the costs for installing solar power systems, with accompanying insurance from an external insurance company. The repayment structure is revenue-based, with 100% of the projected electricity revenue from the generated solar power sold to the Korean Power Exchange (KPX), which will use the produced electricity to repay the loan to IBK. In case of lost revenue, the Korean government fund repays any of the compensation costs to the KPX. This programme covers SME enablers, as well as SME adopters to encourage the take up of solar PV panels.

Market based instruments

Italy: The **Viveracqua Hydrobond** is an innovative financing mechanism developed in Italy to support small and medium-sized water utility companies in raising capital for infrastructure development and modernisation. This covers areas such as improvements to wastewater treatment, as well as water efficiency and distribution upgrades. It is notable for being one of the first cases where mini-bonds were used in the utilities sector, leveraging a pooling structure to achieve efficiencies and attract institutional investors (i.e. used as collateral for an asset-backed securitisation). This financing mechanism is aimed to support eight small and medium-sized water utilities in the Italian region of Veneto. To lower investment risk and reduce financing costs, the mini bonds have received financial backing from public financial institutions, including **EIB** and **Cassa Depositi e Prestiti (CDP).** Five rounds of mini bonds have been issued, following its first successful issuance in 2014.

Sources: (Bpifrance, 2025[5]), (L-Bank, 2025[6]), (NZGIF, 2025[7]), (Business Finland, 2025[8]), (International Energy Agency, 2021[9]), (Indu, 2025[10]), (European Investment Bank, 2014[11]), (CDP, 2022[12]), (EIFO, 2024[13])

Guarantee schemes and other risk-sharing mechanisms facilitate bank lending to SMEs that are delivering green solutions. Unlike standard guarantees, green guarantees are tied specifically to projects with measurable environmental benefits and often come with incentives like reduced fees or technical assistance to promote green investments. In Moldova, for instance, SME renewable energy producers can receive loan guarantees to finance the development and scaling up of their operations (see case study on Moldova in Annex A)

Blended finance combines financing from public and private sources to de-risk high upfront investment costs of green projects or to incentivise the provision and uptake of financing for these types of investments. For example, the Mirova SunFunder Gigaton Fund, a public-private initiative operating in emerging and developing economies, enables the mobilisation of financing for SME generators and providers of solar-generated power (see Box 3.2).

Box 3.2. Examples of risk sharing instruments for enablers

Credit guarantee schemes

Moldova: The Organization for the Development of Entrepreneurship (ODA) in Moldova provided SME renewable energy producers with loan guarantees through its Credit Guarantee Fund. The fund offers guarantees of up to MDL 5 million (EUR 260 000), covering as much as 70% of financing costs. This programme was designed to help renewable energy SMEs access the necessary capital to develop, expand, and scale their operations.

Blended finance

South Africa: The Development Bank of Southern Africa (DBSA), together with the **South African Department of Forestry, Fisheries and Environment (DFFE)** is managing the **Green Fund**. R25 million (EUR 1.25 million) have been allocated to fund project preparation support, feasibility, and technical support, and R70 million (EUR 3.7 million) have been designated for investment funding, with the possibility of raising additional funding from other public and private stakeholders. Funding for projects can go up to 15 years, offering a range of financing instruments, such as grants, equity, loans, and guarantees. Selected projects must have a development impact and can cover domains such as improving wastewater treatment, waste management processes, or renewable energy generation and storage installations, amongst others.

EMDEs: The **Mirova SunFunder Gigaton Fund** is a public-private partnership involving key stakeholders such as the impact investor **Mirova SunFunder, Swedfund**, and the **European Investment Bank (EIB).** The fund mobilises both public and private capital to finance SMEs engaged in clean energy generation and distribution through solar energy projects. With a target size of USD 500 million, the fund aims to unlock private sector investments by leveraging public contributions to de-risk the financing structure. The fund primarily provides medium- to long-term debt financing in emerging markets, with an estimated USD 1.2 billion in private debt funding. It focuses on off-grid SMEs operating in regions with unreliable electricity systems, supporting projects such as solar home systems, agri-solar solutions, and e-mobility initiatives

Sources: (ODA, 2025[14]), (European Investment Bank, 2022[15]), (Development Bank of Southern Africa, 2025[16]).

Supply chain financing facilitates the integration of enablers into supply chains by helping to optimise cash flow within supply chains and allowing suppliers, buyers, and intermediaries to access funds tied up in invoices, purchase orders, or inventory. For SME enablers this type of finance can address critical financing barriers and incentivise sustainability throughout supply chains. Green supply chain financing, which is dedicated to greening activities, can entail many different types of financing including early payment programmes, inventory financing for green products, purchase order financing and sustainability-linked financing. This also includes collaborative financing models whereby public financing providers work with large enterprises/buyers in supply chains to devise programmes for supplier greening, leveraging the buyers' financing or creditworthiness to secure favourable terms for green suppliers. Several examples of green supply chain financing programmes have been included in Box 3.3. For instance, SMEs trading green technologies or services can access long- and short- term trade financing options through the Green Trade Facilitation Programme of the EBRD.

Box 3.3. Examples of trade and supply chain financing for enablers

Canada: Export Development Canada (EDC) is offering trade financing solutions to cleantech SMEs seeking to expand internationally. Support can come in the form of guarantees, loans and working capital. In addition to financial support, the EDC facilitates networking connections through organising Cleantech Export Summits, linking SME enablers with relevant buyers, industry experts, and strategic partners. In 2023, EDC provided CAD 12 billion (USD 9 billion and EUR 8.2 billion) in financing and insurance solutions to more than 440 cleantech companies.

Finland: Finnvera offers export financing on favourable terms to SMEs who are exporting goods and services that meet its climate criteria. Financial incentives can include lower pricing, higher percentage of cover, longer maturity, a more flexible repayment profile or incentives related to collateral requirements or other credit conditions. The climate criteria have been specifically tailored for high-impact sectors such as shipping, energy, and mining. SMEs operating outside these sectors can also benefit from favourable financing terms if they can demonstrate science-based emissions reduction targets aligned with the Paris Agreement.

Spain: The **Spanish Export Credit Agency (CESCE)** offers green trade credit insurance to support SMEs exporting environmentally sustainable products and services. The financing is provided through coverage in the form of buyer credit and supplier credit, ensuring that SMEs can mitigate the risks associated with non-payment in international transactions. The insurance is intended for green projects in sectors such as renewable energy production, sustainable water management, and sustainable mobility.

International: The **EBRD** is unlocking trade financing for high performing green technology and services SMEs through the **Green Trade Facilitation Programme**. Under the programme, the EBRD provides both long term trade financing instruments, such as guarantees in the form of letters of credit and payment guarantees, as well as short term instruments such as loans to partnering banks for on lending to local SME exporters and importers. Since the start of the programme in 2016, the EBRD has provided more than EUR 675 million in green trade finance and facilitated more than 605 000 tonnes of CO_2 in emission savings.

Sources: (EBRD, 2025[17]), (Finnvera, 2025[18]), (EDC, 2025[19]), (CESCE, 2025[20]).

3.2. Non-financial support for enablers

Non-financial support helps SME enablers of the green transition to overcome barriers to scale their products and services and drive the adoption of sustainable practices across industries (Table 3.2). Some of these barriers include:

- **Capacity constraints:** Enablers often face skill and knowledge gaps that limit their ability to scale effectively. Publicly provided non-financial support, such as targeted technical assistance, sector-specific training, or workshops on compliance with environmental standards, can help these SMEs build their internal capacities. For example, Asian and African SMEs working in the renewable energy sector can participate in the Energy Enterprise Coach programme to access tools, best practices and obtain certificates (see case study on the Energy Enterprise Coach in Annex A).
- **Market access:** Enabler SMEs frequently struggle to reach industries or customers that could benefit most from their solutions due to limited visibility, resources, or connections. Additionally, given the highly regulated nature of sectors like renewable energy, they require support in navigating compliance and streamlining approvals. Public support in the form of matchmaking services and digital platforms can help them integrate into supply chains, expand market reach, and access financial institutions. The SOARING programme in Southern Africa for instance helps SMEs to perform due diligence risk assessments to gain market access (see case study on the SOARING Programme in Annex A).
- **Business development services:** These are necessary to address any technical and knowledge skills gap that SME enablers might face. Mentoring, coaching, training, and workshops which teach SME enablers how to scale their solutions and integrate into supply chains are vital. SME enablers also require support on market access, through matchmaking platforms which connect them with relevant partners and consumers (see Box 3.4).

Table 3.2. Non-financial support programmes for SME enablers

Support programme	Description	Examples
Business development services	Assistance in the form of coaching, mentoring, as well as gaining access to training programmes and networks	• Workshops on business models and environmental standards compliance
Market access programmes	Resources such as matchmaking platforms and government-backed marketing campaigns	• Regulatory compliance assistance

Box 3.4. Examples of business development services and market access support programmes for SME enablers

Southern Africa: The **Southern African Renewable Energy Investment and Growth (SOARING)** programme aims to improve financing access for clean energy SMEs who are providing solutions to agricultural value chains, for example through distributing solar-powered water pumps to farmers. The programme provides capacity-building and technical assistance, helping SMEs develop business models, prepare project documentation, and implement due diligence and risk assessment measures to access financing. It also supports local financial institutions in extending green finance products to SMEs through providing credit and risk assessment tools. As such, it bridges the knowledge gap between financial institutions and SMEs, enabling SMEs to access the necessary capital for scaling.

for the Environment, Nature Conservation and Nuclear Safety, and managed by managed by the non-profit organisation **REEEP (Renewable Energy and Energy Efficiency Partnership).**

International: The **Netherlands Enterprise Agency (RVO)** and the **Energising Development (EnDev) partnership** have launched the **Energy Enterprise Coach**, offering capacity training to African and Asian SMEs working in the renewable energy sector. The aim is to foster their growth and development through training, advisory and business development services. The Platform offers an E-Learning Platform with case study examples, tools and assignments. At the end of the course, SME renewable energy generators will obtain a certificate. So far, the programme has had 800 E-learning participants, as well as 500 participants in cohort trainings, and 80 entrepreneurs taking part in individual mentoring programmes.

Sources: (Energy Enterprise Coach, 2025[21]), (REEEP, 2025[22])

3.3. References

Bpifrance (2025), *ADEME anaerobic digestion loan*, https://www.bpifrance.fr/catalogue-offres/pret-methanisation-ademe. [5]

Business Finland (2025), *Investment aid for Circular Economy*, https://www.businessfinland.fi/en/for-finnish-customers/services/funding/investment-aid-for-circular-economy. [8]

CDP (2022), *A new Hydrobond for Viveracqua*, https://www.cdp.it/sitointernet/page/en/a_new_hydrobond_for_viveracqua?contentId=PRG41790. [12]

CESCE (2025), *New green policies on behalf of the State*, https://www.cesce.fr/en/web/guest/cuenta-del-estado/polizas-verdes. [20]

Development Bank of Southern Africa (2025), *Green Fund*, https://www.dbsa.org/solutions/climate-financing/green-fund. [16]

EBRD (2025), *Facts, figures and Green TFP*, https://tfp-ebrd.com/. [17]

EDC (2025), *Cleantech at EDC*, https://www.edc.ca/cleantech. [19]

EIFO (2024), *Green Accelerator*, https://www.eifo.dk/en/our-solutions/green-accelerator/. [13]

Energy Enterprise Coach (2025), *Energy Enterprise Coach*, https://ee-coach.com/. [21]

European Commission (2016), *Guidebook Series How to support SME Policy from Structural Funds. Improving Resource Efficiency in SMEs*. [1]

European Investment Bank (2022), *SUNFUNDER GIGATON CLEAN ENERGY SME FUND.*, https://www.eib.org/fr/projects/all/20220074. [15]

European Investment Bank (2014), *VIVERACQUA HYDROBOND*, https://www.eib.org/fr/projects/all/20130515. [11]

Finnvera (2025), *Climate criteria for export financing*, https://www.finnvera.fi/eng/export-and-internationalisation/finnvera-as-an-export-finance-provider/climate-criteria-for-export-financing. [18]

Global Partnership for Financial Inclusion (2017), *Financing for SMEs in Sustainable Global Value Chains*. [4]

Indu (2025), *Consultation with Industrial Bank of Korea*. [10]

International Energy Agency (2021), *Uttar Pradesh Mini-Grid Policy 2016*, https://www.iea.org/policies/6374-uttar-pradesh-mini-grid-policy-2016. [9]

L-Bank (2025), *Energie vom Land – Sonne, Wind, Wasser*, https://www.l-bank.de/produkte/wirtschaftsfoerderung/energie-vom-land-sonne-wind-wasser.html. [6]

NZGIF (2025), *NZGIF Green Finance Accelerator*, https://www.nzgif.co.nz/investing/nzgif-green-finance-accelerator. [7]

ODA (2025), *What is the ODA Credit Guarantee Fund (CGF)?*, https://www.oda.md/en/access-to-finance/credit-guarantee-fund. [14]

OECD (2023), *SME and Entrepreneurship Outlook 2023*. [3]

REEEP (2025), *SOARING (Southern African Renewable Energy Investment and Growth)*, https://reeep.org/projects_programmes/soaring/. [22]

SWITCH2Green (2025), *Green Action Plan for SMEs - Turning environmental challenges into business opportunities*. [2]

4 SME adopters: Financial and non-financial support mechanisms

This chapter examines the financial and non-financial support mechanisms for SMEs integrating sustainable practices into their operations. Drawing on a range of instruments such as green loans, green leases, property-linked financing, blended finance and performance-based models, it showcases how public and private actors can facilitate SMEs investments in energy efficiency, renewable energy, and resource optimisation. In addition to financing, the chapter explores non-financial measures, such as advisory services, awareness-raising campaigns, technical training and support for environmental management systems and certifications, which help SMEs identify opportunities for greening and strengthen their capacity to implement sustainable solutions.

Most SMEs world-wide need to adopt greener technologies and business practices to align with the growing focus on sustainability in the global economy. This includes SMEs with vastly different characteristics, ranging from microenterprises with 10 or fewer employees who are providing essential services to consumers in local communities, to medium-sized companies embedded in complex supply chains with increasingly stringent demands on sustainability performance. As such, these diverse enterprises need access to a wide range of financing and capacity buildings solutions to meet their greening needs.

Tailored green and sustainable financing support is critical for enabling SMEs to transition toward greener and more sustainable practices. By enabling the financing of investments in greening, notably through direct financing and risk sharing support, and by rewarding progress toward environmental targets through better financing conditions, these financing instruments and programmes have a key role to play in facilitating SMEs' investments in resource efficiency, decarbonisation, and sustainable growth.

Non-financial support from public entities is essential in facilitating SME greening by addressing barriers beyond access to capital. Many SMEs, for instance, lack the technical knowledge, skills, and capacity required to implement sustainable practices or leverage green finance effectively. Public entities can provide targeted assistance through capacity-building programs, such as training and workshops, to improve SMEs' understanding of sustainability strategies, environmental regulations, and market opportunities. Advisory services and resource centres can further guide SMEs in areas like decarbonisation, resource efficiency, and obtaining of green certifications.

Public entities also play a critical role in fostering the uptake of green and sustainable finance among SMEs through non-financial support. By raising awareness of available financing instruments and their benefits, public entities can help SMEs understand how tools like green and sustainability-linked loans and blended finance can align with their business goals and facilitate their investments in necessary greening technologies and processes.

Non-financial support can also help SMEs strengthen their capacities to meet sustainability measurement and reporting requirements, which are increasingly essential for accessing green and sustainable finance and participating in sustainable supply chains. Many SMEs lack the technical expertise and resources to track, measure, and report on environmental and social performance in line with evolving standards and regulations (G20SFWG, 2024[1]). Public entities can provide capacity-building initiatives, such as training programs and workshops, to help SMEs understand sustainability metrics, reporting frameworks, and data collection processes. Additionally, advisory services and digital tools can simplify compliance by offering step-by-step guidance and ready-to-use templates tailored to SME needs. The OECD has developed a *Guidance Note on fostering convergence in SME sustainability reporting*, providing a core set of sustainability indicators and metrics that SMEs can refer to report on their sustainability performance (Kuzmanovic, Koreen and Honegger, 2025[2])

4.1. Financial support for SME adopters

Financing solutions for these actors need to serve several important purposes, which can vary in importance depending on the specific characteristics of the enterprise:

- **Reducing up-front costs:** Investing in greening technologies comes with high up-front costs, which can be prohibitive particularly for smaller businesses. In fact, high upfront costs are often cited as a key constraint for greening by SMEs. For instance, in a 2023 survey of over 6000 SMEs in 13 countries globally, 68% stated that greening is too costly to implement and 51% identified specifically the cost of green technologies as a key constraint for greening (International Chamber of Commerce, 2024[...]). The cost of environmental actions was also cited as the second largest

Commission, 2024[4]). Financial support that can help reduce the upfront investment costs of SMEs through, for example. grants, loans, subsidies or tax incentives[1] – can make the difference between SMEs investing in greening or not.

- **Reducing financing and investment-related risk for SMEs**: Public financial support can help reduce the financial risks associated with SME investments in greening. Transitioning to sustainable practices often involves uncertainty, such as fluctuating energy prices, evolving regulations, or unproven technologies. By offering risk-sharing mechanisms like loan guarantees, blended finance or green insurance schemes, public financial support can mitigate these risks, encouraging SMEs to adopt environmentally friendly technologies or practices. Studies show that risk aversion is a key barrier to SME green investments with many SMEs fearing potential financial losses if these investments do not yield the expected returns (OECD, 2021[5]). In a UK survey, for instance, 19% of small businesses cited insufficient returns on green investments as a significant obstacle to taking such actions. Furthermore, nearly 50% of small businesses cited cost as a challenge and only 25% believed that investing in sustainability results in some or substantial savings (Small Business Britain, 2024[6]).
- **Reducing financial risk for financing providers**: Public financial support can also play a pivotal role in reducing the financial risks for institutions financing SMEs' green investments. Financial institutions often perceive lending to SMEs for sustainable projects as high-risk due to uncertainties around project viability, limited collateral, and potential market volatility. These compound traditional financing constraints for SMEs such as information asymmetries, high administrative costs relative to the size of the financing, etc. (OECD, 2022[7]). Public interventions, such as green credit guarantees, co-financing schemes, or first-loss provisions, can help de-risk these investments by sharing potential losses and enhancing the creditworthiness of SMEs. This not only incentivises financial institutions to provide more capital for SME greening but also fosters the development of tailored financial products for sustainability-related investments. Research indicates that de-risking mechanisms significantly improve credit flow to SMEs, bridging the financing gap and accelerating the transition to greener economies (Asian Development Bank Institute, 2018[8]).

A broad range of financing solutions can be used to enable SMEs' adoption of greening solutions and practices. These instruments can be classified in seven broad categories including direct and indirect financing instruments, such as green loans and leases; risk-sharing instruments, such as loan guarantees and blended finance instruments; incentive-based instruments, such as grants and subsidies; performance-based instruments, including energy performance contracts; market-based instruments, such as bonds and carbon credits; sustainability-linked instruments, including loans and mini bonds; and trade finance instruments for green goods and services, including supply chain financing (see Table 4.1).

Table 4.1. Common financial support options for SMEs adopters of green solutions

Instrument	Description	Examples
Direct financing instruments		
Green loans	Financing offering preferential interest rates or other more favourable financing conditions for sustainable investments. Can be provided directly or indirectly via credit lines	• Energy efficiency loans for upgrading machinery • Loans for retrofitting buildings • Financing for installation of small-scale renewable infrastructure (e.g. solar panels, water saving equipment) • Loans for purchasing of EVs & related infrastructure
Green leases	Instruments that incorporate environmental clauses into leasing agreements, allowing SMEs to access environmentally friendly energy equipment or technologies for buildings without bearing the high upfront costs	• Leases for green technology including energy-efficient equipment and renewable energy • Leases for green building upgrades: • Leases for electric vehicle (EV) purchases • Leases for EV infrastructure (e.g. EV charging

		stations and related infrastructure for businesses) • Sustainability-focused tenant improvement leases
Property-linked loans (PPLs)	Loans designed for environmental property refurbishments, tied to the property rather than the borrower, with repayment integrated into property taxes.	• PPLs for upgrading energy efficiency of property • PPLs for installing renewable energy systems on property • PPLs for improving water efficiency of property
Green revenue-based loans	Financing whereby repayment terms are tied to revenues generated from green projects	• Solar panel installation loans where repayment is structured around generated savings • Loans for installation of green technologies which convert waste into renewable energy where repayment is a percentage of the energy revenue generated
Risk sharing instruments		
Green guarantees	Financing mechanisms providing a financial backstop that ensures partial repayment to lenders if an SME defaults, reducing the risk for private lenders. Green guarantees offer more favourable financing terms than other guarantee instruments.	• Guarantees to financial intermediaries to provide financing at favourable terms to SMEs adopting green machinery and equipment
Blended finance	Strategic use of public or philanthropic capital to de-risk investments and attract private capital into projects that deliver environmental benefits.	• Concessional loans paired with grant or technical assistance components • Viability-gap-funding, where grants make the financing of the rest of the project viable for private sector partners
Green synthetic securitisation	Credit risk of a portfolio of loans is transferred to third-party investors using credit derivatives or guarantee. The existing portfolio and/or the new lending (use-or-proceeds) is green.	• Financing for climate friendly investments such as clean energy transport technologies
Incentive-based instruments		
Grants and subsidies	Non-repayable financing in the form of lump sum or recurring payments that can help SMEs cover high upfront costs of greening investments	• Grants for purchasing renewable energy systems or energy-efficient equipment • Subsidies to offset operational costs of green investments/processes • Subsidies/grants for improving energy efficiency of buildings • Subsidies to calculate environmental footprint of goods & services
Performance-based financing instruments		
Energy Performance Contracts (EPCs):	Instruments where repayment is tied to energy cost savings achieved through efficiency improvements	• Energy efficiency upgrade of manufacturing equipment, where energy savings provide repayments • Energy-efficiency LED bulbs retrofit
Pay-as-you-save models	Financing where repayments are directly linked to savings generated by green technologies, such as solar panels or efficient HVAC systems.	• Installment of energy-efficient HVAC system • Insultation and window upgrades with generated savings providing repayment
Market-based instruments		
Green bonds	Debt issued by financial institutions or SMEs to finance greening investments as well mini bonds issued by SMEs themselves. Differs from other bonds in terms of financing conditions and premia for green performance.	• Bonds issued by PFIs or MDBs to raise capital for financing SME green projects, like renewable energy installations. • Mini bonds issued by SMEs themselves to finance greening projects
Sustainability-linked instruments		
Sustainability-linked loans	Loans where interest rates are tied to the sustainability performance of the entity	• Loans with interest rates that decrease if SMEs meet predefined sustainability performance targets (SPTs), like reducing waste by a certain percentage or transitioning to renewable energy. • Sustainability-linked supply chain financing

Green Trade Finance	Reduces the risk for exporters and importers of green goods, services, and technology. Facilitates SME participation in green supply chains through mechanisms for easing cash flow challenges or de-risking transactions	• Guarantees and letters of credit for green trade transactions • Supply chain financing for producing energy efficient equipment • Short term trade loans for the import or export of green goods and services • Accounts payable and receivable financing for buyers and exporters of green goods

Direct or indirect financing instruments provide capital to SMEs for purchasing or adopting green technologies and processes. These instruments can include:

Green loans support SMEs in financing environmentally sustainable projects, such as renewable energy installations, energy-efficient upgrades, or waste reduction initiatives. These loans often feature more competitive or subsidised financing costs and more flexible terms to incentivise SMEs' investments in actions that reduce their environmental footprint and promote long-term cost savings. For instance, in Czechia, long-term interest-free loans are provided to SMEs for building retrofits with options to convert energy savings into financing to reduce the loan principal (see case study on the ENERG programme in Czechia in Annex A).

Green loans can vary in maturity depending on the SMEs' financing needs:

- Short-term loans typically have repayment periods of less than a year and are used to address working capital needs, manage cash flow, or cover operational costs. In the context of greening, short-term loans can help SMEs finance immediate, smaller-scale green initiatives such as energy-efficient equipment upgrades, installing solar panels, or adopting waste-reduction technologies. Several examples of this kind of financing are included in Box 4.1. Under its flagship Multiple beneficiary intermediated loan (MBIL) programme, for example, the European Investment Bank (EIB) offers various green financing products for SMEs, including working capital financing, leasing and others, that are provided through intermediary banks.
- Medium- and long-term loans, on the other hand, are often used to finance investments that require more substantial capital outlays and generate returns over a longer period. For SMEs, medium- and long-term loans can finance endeavours like transitioning to sustainable supply chain practices, implementing renewable energy solutions, other infrastructure development, or extensive operational transformations. For example, Indian SMEs can access medium-term financing provided by the Small Industries Development Bank of India (SIDB) for capital intensive investments in clean energy and energy efficiency measures. The funding is provided on favourable terms, collateral free and with reduced interest rates (2.5% below the market interest rate) and covers up to 90% of the project costs (see Box 4.1). Likewise, Mexican SMEs can purchase energy-efficient equipment through a medium-term loan provided by the Sustainable Eco Credit programme, which also covers the costs of external consulting services to assist SMEs in selecting the most suitable equipment (see case study from the Nacional Financiera in Mexico in Annex A).

Green loans can also vary depending on the mode of provision. Funding can be extended directly from the public development bank to the SME clients or provided indirectly via credit lines through relevant public or private intermediaries. For instance, the Green Economic Financing Facility (GEFF) of the European Bank of Reconstruction and Development (EBRD)[2] issues green credit lines to partnering financial institutions in Central and Eastern Europe, Central Asia, the Southern and Eastern Mediterranean, and some parts of Sub-Saharan Africa, to facilitate lending to SMEs for investments in energy efficiency, renewable energy, water savings, and waste reduction. The funding is provided at competitive interest rates and repayment terms often tailored to the local market. Some GEFF programs also include incentive grants (e.g., cashbacks) funded by donors or other international organisations for completed and verified green investments (see Box 4.1).

Green leasing products help SMEs adopt sustainable practices by providing access to eco-friendly equipment, technologies, or vehicles without requiring significant upfront investment and by spreading costs through periodic lease payments. Green leases often include favourable terms or incentives for green solutions and are often provided by private entities with public support in the form of risk sharing mechanisms (see Box 4.1). For example, in Germany, the state-owned development bank KfW provides financing to leasing companies, which in turn offer favourable leasing terms to SMEs and self-employed professionals for acquiring new corporate equipment and vehicles to improve sustainability performance (see Box 4.1).

Property-linked loans enable SMEs to finance sustainable property upgrades, such as energy-efficient retrofits or renewable energy systems, by linking the loan to the property rather than the business. This approach makes it easier to transfer the loan if the property is sold, incentivising green investments while reducing the financial risk for SMEs. Examples of such financing programmes include the Environmental Upgrade Finance scheme in Australia, which finances the installation of energy and water efficiency upgrades, renewable energy installations and waste minimisation projects in industrial and commercial buildings. Under this programme, property owners receive upfront 100% of the financing for approved projects and the repayment is conducted over a term of up to 20 years. Repayments are made through the local council rate systems, with generated energy savings being able to offset repayments (see case study on Australia in Annex A).

Box 4.1. Examples of direct financing instruments for adopters

Green loans

Australia: The **Clean Energy Finance Corporation (CEFC)** is collaborating with the **National Australia Bank** in implementing the **Equipment Finance – Energy Efficiency Bonus programme.** It provides favourable financing for energy efficient upgrades such as upgrading vehicles to EVs, improving equipment or increasing the use of renewable energy. Financing can range from AUD 10 000 (USD 6 200 and EUR 5 600) to AUD 5 million (USD 3.1 million and EUR 2.8 million), with a 0.7% discount on NAB's standard equipment financing rate. Repayment periods can go up to 10 years. The programme commenced in 2015 with an initial investment of AUD 120 million (USD 74.4 million and EUR 67.2 million) from the CEFC. By 2017, the programme had already financed more than 1,000 clean energy assets in Australia. Strong uptake was noted especially amongst agribusiness customers, using the loans to finance equipment upgrades, especially in the area of the Great Barrier Reef. Due to its strong uptake, the CEFC provided an additional investment of AUD 180 million in 2017.

Czechia: The National Development Bank is providing interest-free green loans under its **'Energ'** programme to SMEs in Prague implementing energy-saving projects. This primarily includes building retrofitting measures, such as reconstructing electricity and gas distribution systems or replacing air conditioning systems. The interest-free loans are long term, with repayment periods of up to 10 years, and can amount to a maximum of CZK 60 million (USD 2.7 million and EUR 2.4 million) covering up to 70% of the project costs. The programme features a mechanism whereby generated energy savings from implemented projects can later be converted into a financial contribution, which can reduce the loan principal by up to 7%. The costs for conducting the energy savings assessment can also be partially subsidised by the programme.

Chile: The national development bank, **Banco Estado**, offers **Ecomobility Loans** tailored for SMEs to support the acquisition of new electric vehicles and the development of associated charging infrastructure. These loans can cover up to 100% of financing costs and feature preferential terms, including reduced interest rates and extended repayment periods of up to 20 years.

Greece: The **Hellenic Development Bank (HDB)** is providing **Green Co-Financing loans** through participating financial intermediaries to SMEs who are implementing energy transition projects. Eligible projects include green mobility, energy efficiency or renewable energy projects. The total programme portfolio is EUR 415 million. SMEs benefit from a 40% interest-free capital contribution, while the remaining 60% is financed by financial intermediaries with interest rates subsidised by HDB up to 2%.

India: Indian SMEs in manufacturing and services can access financing under the **'4E Scheme – End to End Energy Efficiency'** by the **Small Industries Development Bank of India** for capital-intensive projects which aim to increase energy efficiency and renewable energy use, like solar panel installations or energy-saving technology. The scheme offers medium-term loans repayable in 5 years (extendable to 7), covering up to 90% of the project cost without collateral requirements, at a maximum amount of Rs. 7.5 crore (USD 903 600 and EUR 825 000). Indian MSMEs benefit from concessional financing of about 2.5% below the market lending rate. The scheme further offers a subsidised technical consultant service for conducting energy audits and implementation support.

Mexico: The **Eco Sustainable Credit Programme** by the **Nacional Financiera (NAFIN)** helps SMEs transition to a low carbon economy. The programme is implemented in collaboration with the **Ministry of Finance and Public Credit (SHCP)** and the **Ministry of Environment and Natural Resources (SEMARNAT).** SMEs can access loans on favourable terms of up to MXN 15 million (USD 825 000 and EUR 700 000) to finance the purchase of energy-efficient and renewable energy machinery, with a repayment period of up to 8 years. The programme fully subsidises the cost of an energy audit through a partnering company, enabling SMEs to select the most suitable equipment. Over the course of two years, 1 000 projects have been implemented, leading to a reduction of 100 000 tons of CO2e.

Sweden: Swedish SMEs can access **green loans** from the public development bank **Almi** for projects such as energy efficiency improvements, building retrofits, and heat pump installations. These loans offer favourable terms, including extended repayment periods of up to 10 years and lower interest rates. The loans are backed by **InvestEU guarantees** and projects must be in line with requirements inspired by the EU's Sustainable Taxonomy to qualify for financing. SMEs can book a free meeting to discuss their investment plans and assess eligibility.

Thailand: The Small and Medium Enterprise Development Bank of Thailand (SME D Bank) is providing support to SMEs and entrepreneurs through its **SME Green Productivity loans.** Eligible activities include the installation of clean energy systems or the purchase of equipment that enhances environmental performance. The programme offers reduced interest rates fixed at 3% per year for the first three years with a maximum amount of THB 10 million (USD 280 000 and EUR 255 000). Additionally, borrowers benefit from a 12-month grace period on principal repayments.

Türkiye: The **World Bank** has implemented the **Türkiye Green Industry Project** in partnership with the **Ministry of Industry and Technology, Small and Medium Enterprises Development Organization of Türkiye (KOSGEB)** and the **Scientific and Technological Research Council of Türkiye (TÜBITAK).** The USD 450 million project supports Turkish industrial SMEs in adopting green and sustainable practices. KOSGEB provides 250 million in reimbursable support to SMEs for green practices such as solar panel installations, circular economy, and resource efficiency initiatives. The programme offers support for up to 12 months, covering 60% to 70% of eligible costs, including machinery, equipment, software and personnel expenses.

Africa: The **International Fund for Agricultural Development (IFAD**) is offering green loans and grants to agricultural SMEs in Africa who are implementing environmentally friendly practices into their operations through the **Inclusive Green Financing Initiative (IGREENFIN I).** The programme consists of three components, a "Green Business Financing Facility" that will provide funds for on-lending to select Local National Agricultural Banks (LNABs), a technical assistance component, and a regional support programme to increase learning and innovation across the region.

Europe: The **EIB Group** is helping agricultural SMEs in becoming more sustainable through the **Pan-European agricultural programme**, with a total funding capacity of EUR 3 billion. This initiative offers loans for both investments and working capital, with SMEs able to borrow up to EUR 25 million. The funding can cover 50% to 100% of project costs, and loans come with flexible repayment terms of up to 15 years. The funding can further be backed by guarantees provided by the EIF. Eligible projects include those focused on sustainable and regenerative agriculture, water management systems, integration of renewable energy, sustainable aquaculture, and resource efficiency measures.

International: The **European Bank for Reconstruction and Development** (EBRD), provides indirect green lending to SMEs adopting green technologies through partnering financial intermediaries under the **Green Economy Financing Facility (GEFF)**. This initiative combines financing with technical assistance to identify eligible green technologies focused on energy efficiency, renewable energy, water savings, and waste reduction. The green credit lines are mainly going to emerging markets - spanning 29 countries - with funding of EUR 6.3 billion. The funding is provided at competitive interest rates and repayment terms often tailored to the local market. Some GEFF programs include incentive grants (e.g., cashbacks) funded by donors or other international organisations for completed and verified green investments. The projects have so far prevented the release of an estimated 10 million tonnes of CO_2 emissions into the atmosphere.

Green leasing products

Germany: The public development bank **KfW** offers the **Sustainable ERP Global Loan-Leasing Programme** to support SMEs in financing energy-efficient and sustainable investments. KfW extends global loans to partner leasing companies enabling them to provide competitive leasing options to end-users for leasing equipment such as energy-efficient machinery, green mobility, and renewable energy technologies. The programme offers favourable interest rates and flexible repayment terms.

Portugal: The Banco Português de Fomento (BPF) is offering indirect financing to Portuguese SMEs through its **Credit Line for Decarbonization and Circular Economy Programme,** aimed at fostering sustainable business practices. Eligible projects include initiatives related to energy efficiency, circular economy, and renewable energy infrastructure. SMEs can access financing of up to EUR 2 million by submitting a request through participating credit institutions, which evaluate the project and provide funding under the program's favourable terms. Beneficiaries can take advantage of subsidised interest rates at 1.5%, with long repayment periods of up to 10 years.

South Africa: The Industrial Development Corporation is encouraging South African SMEs to implement renewable energy and energy efficiency projects into their business. The **Green Energy Efficiency Fund (GEEF)** is a R 500 million fund (USD 28.5 million and EUR 25.9 million) launched in 2011, designed to support SMEs in achieving energy savings and reducing emissions. Loans range from R 1 million (USD 56 900 and EUR 51 700) to R 5 million (USD 2.86 million and EUR 2.6 million) and must be paid back within 15 years. These loans are offered at an interest rate of prime minus 2%. SMEs can further benefit from accompanying technical support, including an energy assessment of the proposed project. This assessment helps to mitigate investment risk by evaluating the expected economic and financial benefits of the project and providing guidance on selecting the appropriate

International: A public-private partnership between the **European Investment Bank (EIB) and Deutsche Leasing** provides **green leases** to SMEs and midcaps in Germany and Eastern Europe. The initiative supports the acquisition of green technology, energy-efficient machinery, and low-carbon mobility solutions. The programme offers flexible repayment terms and competitive interest rates, benefitting SMEs who wish to adopt more sustainable technologies but lack the capital to cover high upfront costs. The project has mobilised EUR 560 million, with the EIB contributing EUR 200 million and 30% allocated to green leases.

Property-linked loans

Australia: The **Environmental Upgrade Finance** scheme helps SMEs who own properties to install energy-efficient and renewable energy upgrades without affecting cash flow. Eligible upgrades include energy efficient technology, renewable energy systems, water saving technologies and sustainable building materials. The loans are linked to the property, covering up to 100% of the financing with no need for upfront capital or additional security. Repayments are long-term and collected through local council rate systems. This programme benefits SMEs who want to make sustainable upgrades to their buildings without having to pay high upfront capital costs. The sustainable building upgrades will help SMEs reduce energy costs in the long-term.

United States: The **Property Assessed Clean Energy (PACE)** programme in the US enabled the installation of energy-efficient HVAC systems, solar panels, insulation, and water conservation measures in residential and commercial properties. SMEs had to own the property to access this funding. Under this programme, property owners received upfront 100% of the financing for approved projects and the repayment was conducted over a term of up to 20 years through additional charges (repayment instalments + interest) on the property tax bill. Since the repayment obligation was tied to the property rather than the individual, if the property was sold, the remaining repayment obligations typically stayed with the property (and the new owner) rather than following the seller. The programme also sought to make the upgrades cost-neutral or even profitable for the owner over time with growing energy savings, as those savings could partially or fully offset the additional costs in the annual tax bills. PACE programs often included educational resources for property owners to help them understand the benefits, obligations, and process of participating in PACE financing. Many PACE programs provided training for contractors to ensure they are knowledgeable about eligible improvements, program requirements, and consumer protection standards. The programme ended in 2025.

Sources: (National Development Bank Czechia, 2025[9]), (Small Industries Development Bank of India, 2025[10]), (BancoEstado, 2025[11]), (Almi, 2025[12]), (Clean Energy Finance Corporation, 2015[13]), (Nacional Financiera, 2025[14]), (European Bank for Reconstruction and Development, 2025[15]), (Kreditanstalt für Wiederaufbau, 2025[16]), (European Investment Bank, 2024[17]), (U.S Department of Energy, 2025[18]), (Sustainability Victoria, 2025[19]), (World Bank, 2024[20]), (Banco Português de Fomento, 2025[21]), (Industrial Development Corporation, 2025[22]), (Hellenic Development Bank, 2025[23]), (IFAD, 2025[24]), (Money and Banking, 2024[25]), (EIB Group, 2024[26])

Risk sharing instruments, such as green guarantees and green insurance products (see Table 4.1), help reduce the financial risks for both SMEs and financial institutions involved in greening investments. Green risk-sharing instruments differ from non-green ones by specifically targeting projects that deliver environmental benefits. As a result, they can provide more favourable terms and can come with additional technical or capacity building support. Common green and sustainable risk-sharing instruments include:

Green guarantees provide a financial backstop, ensuring partial repayment to lenders if the SME defaults on its repayment obligations. Unlike standard guarantees, green guarantees are tied specifically to projects with measurable environmental benefits and often come with incentives like reduced fees or technical assistance to promote green investments.

Guarantees can differ based on their structure and purpose. In the case of direct or indirect financing instruments for SMEs, the most common guarantee instruments include loan guarantees, whereby a portion of the repayment to lenders is guaranteed for loans directed at green projects. Some examples of these kinds of financing products are included in Box 4.2. In Mexico, for instance, he Fideicomisos Instituidos en la Relación con la Agricultura (FIRA), supports agricultural SMEs with loan guarantees covering 40% to 80% of the amount, offering higher coverage for underserved groups like women, youth, and indigenous producers. Complementary non-financial support is provided in the form of technical assistance, training, and project validation support. In Europe, the InvestEU Sustainability Guarantee provides financial intermediaries with guarantees which cover up to 70% of losses to unlock financing under favourable conditions to SMEs who are undergoing green initiatives (see case study on the InvestEU Sustainability Guarantee in Annex A)

Blended finance combines public, philanthropic, and private capital to reduce risks and improve the viability of sustainable investments. As noted, SME adopters often face challenges with upfront costs and limited access to affordable financing. Blended finance can address these issues by leveraging concessional funding—such as grants, subsidies, or first loss guarantees—to lower investment risks and attract private capital. The combination of loans and grants is also helpful for incentivising financing of investments that are not capable of generating sufficient economic returns or cost savings to be viable without additional support, and it can help stimulate both the supply and demand for such financing and investment. Examples of such instruments are included in Box 4.2

In Poland, for example, the Ecological Credit Programme provided by the public development bank Bank Gospodarstwa Krajowego (BGK) enables Polish SMEs to enhance energy efficiency in their operations through blended financing incorporating green credit and a non-refundable grant. The programme includes the provision of credit lines to intermediary banks, which can be used to finance up to 100% of projects' costs. This funding is combined with a so-called "ecological bonus" in the form of a non-refundable grant that can repay up to 80% of the loan's principal (the actual amount is determined by BKG and the intermediary bank depending on the size of the enterprise, its location and the subject of the investment).

Green synthetic securitisations enable financial intermediaries to free up more capital for green financing. Green loans are pooled and the credit risk of the loan portfolio is transferred to and covered by a third party. For example, in Europe, DNB, a Norwegian commercial lender, together with the EIB group, is offering financing through green synthetic securitisation to Nordic SMEs who are investing in clean transportation. The EIB group provides credit risk protection on the DNB's loan portfolio, through the process of Significant Risk Transfer, unlocking more capital for the DNB to allocate to green financing (see the EIB-DNB case study in Annex A).

Box 4.2. Examples of risk sharing instruments

Green guarantees

France: the public development bank **Bpifrance** is offering a **Green Development Guarantee** to projects related to the ecological and energy transition. Eligible projects include energy efficient technologies, renewable energy solutions, waste reduction initiatives and production of eco-friendly products and services. The guarantee can cover various financing instruments such as medium to long term loans, leasing agreements, as well as financial leasing, with a guarantee rate of up to 80%.

Mexico: The Fideicomisos Instituidos en la Relación con la Agricultura (FIRA) is offering guarantees to SMEs who are operating in the agricultural sector and implementing sustainability measures into their practices. The guarantee coverage can vary depending on the specific program to 80% of the loan amount, with higher coverage ratios potentially available for underserved groups such as women, youth, and indigenous producers. In addition to financial guarantees, FIRA offers technical assistance, training, and technology-transfer support to agricultural SMEs. FIRA also assists SMEs in the validation of sustainable projects by covering validation expenses and offering specialized technical advice at no cost. This support includes the preparation of technical documents required by validating entities and assistance in interactions with financial intermediaries to expedite credit evaluations and eligibility assessments.

Thailand: The **Small Industrial Credit Guarantee Corporation (TCG)** is providing guarantees on the SME Green Productivity loans provided by the **Small and Medium Enterprise Development Bank of Thailand (SME D Bank).** TCG can guarantee loans of up to THB 40 million (USD 1.2 million and EUR 1 million) per SME, with an annual guarantee fee of 1.5%, waived for the first four years. The guarantee mechanism is expected to facilitate access to finance for SMEs, unlocking over 300 additional loans to support green investments.

Africa: The **Green Guarantee Facility**, provided by the **Nordic Development Fund** and the **African Guarantee Fund,** is offering guarantees for financing SME green projects in the domains of sustainable energy, sustainable agriculture, resource management and green services. Guarantees can be provided in the form of loan guarantees, equity guarantees and green fundraising guarantees. The guarantee coverage rate can go up to 75% and the programme offers accompanying capacity building support to both financial institutions and SMEs.

EU: The **EU,** under the **InvestEU Sustainability Guarantee programme** implemented by the **European Investment Fund (EIF),** is offering guarantees to financial intermediaries, such as banks and other types of financial institutions, across the EU to provide favourable green debt financing to SMEs that are enablers, innovators and adopters of green technologies. The guarantee supports sustainable investments as per the criteria of the EU Taxonomy, targeting key areas such as climate change mitigation and adaptation, the circular economy, and biodiversity protection, among others, covering up to 70% of the potential losses. The guarantee facility enables SMEs to access favourable financing terms, such as lower interest rates, reduced collateral requirements and longer loan tenures. Additionally, it includes an advisory tool, the Sustainability Guarantee Tool, to assist implementation, offering financial intermediaries and SMEs support in assessing project eligibility and estimating the climate impact of investments.

Blended finance

Germany: In Germany, **KfW** offers loans to SMEs to finance the construction or renovation of energy efficient buildings through the **CO2 emission reduction loan programme**. Loans are provided by commercial banks with a repayment period of up to 10 years and an interest rate subsidy and capital rebate, based on the energy savings achieved. The rebate can reach up to 27.5% for renovations and 50% for new constructions. In practice, the rebate reduces the loan tenor by writing off the final annuities owed by the borrower. This effectively shortens the repayment period for the recipient.

Poland: The Bank Gospodarstwa Krajowego (BGK) provides the **Ecological Credit Programme**, designed to support SMEs in implementing energy efficiency measures in their buildings and operations. Eligible projects include investments aimed at improving energy efficiency by at least 30%, such as modernisation of machinery andthermo-modernization of buildings, and installation of renewable energy sources (RES). The programme includes the provision of credit lines to intermediary banks, which can be used to finance up to 100% of projects' costs. This funding is combined with a so-called "ecological bonus" in the form of a non-refundable grant that can repay up to 80% of the loan's principal (the actual amount is determined by BKG and the intermediary bank depending on the size of the enterprise, its location and the subject of the investment). A total of PLN 1.32 billion (USD 303.6

million and EUR 290 million) is allocated for co-financing under the programme, with the grants funded by the European Union.

Slovakia: In Slovakia, SMEs who are implementing renewable energy or energy efficiency projects can access funding from the **SlovSEFF III (Slovak Sustainable Energy Financing Facility).** The programme is a collaboration between the **EBRD, Ministry of Environment of the Slovak Republic** and **the Ministry of Agriculture, Food and Environment of Spain**. The SlovSEFF III offers credit lines to local banks, who pass them on as loans to SMEs implementing sustainable energy projects. The programme incentivises GHG emission reductions through linking a project's GHG emission reduction potential to incentive payments, which are financed by carbon credit transactions between the Slovakian and Spanish governments. Loans are combined with capital grants ranging from 5% to 20% of the loan amount. Participating SMEs can further benefit from technical assistance, such as receiving support for conducting energy audits and calculating GHG emissions.

Africa: A public-private initiative, the **Africa Agriculture and Trade Investment Fund (AATIF)** provides financing to agricultural SMEs who are implementing sustainable practices. Financing is provided both in direct form, providing loans or equity to African agribusinesses, or indirectly, providing funding to financial intermediaries, who pass it onto agricultural SMEs. The fund employs a first-loss structure, with public financial institutions absorbing initial losses to encourage private sector participation. Investments must meet the IFC's Performance Standards on Environmental and Social Sustainability to be eligible. AATIF also includes a Technical Assistance Programme that offers grant-based support to help projects achieve their development goals. The fund, totalling USD 146 million, is backed by key public institutions such as the **KfW, the German Ministry for Economic Development and Cooperation (BMZ), the United Nations Environment Programme (UNEP) and the International Labour Organization (ILO).**

Green synthetic securitisation

The Nordics: DNB Bank ASA (DNB) and the **EIB group** are providing EUR 190 million to fund SMEs' green initiatives. Eligible projects include leasing clean energy vehicles and investing in clean transport technologies (e.g.in the construction sector). The funding is facilitated through synthetic green securitisation, with the EIB Group offering credit protection on DNB's EUR 1.5 billion loan portfolio. This arrangement allows DNB to free up additional capital and tooffer SMEs more favourable financing conditions for undertaking green initiatives. The EIF provides credit risk protection to DNB on the mezzanine tranche of EUR 95 million, which is then counter-guaranteed by the EIB. This structure ensures that the EIB Group assumes the mezzanine tranche risk of the referenced portfolio. Key features of the transaction include synthetic excess spread, a replenishment period, as well as a pro-rata amortisation of both the senior and mezzanine tranches, subject to performance triggers.

Sources: (European Investment Fund (EIF), 2025[27]), (Bpifrance, 2025[28]), (Gobierno de Mexico, 2025[29]), (Nordic Development Fund, 2025[30]), (BGK, 2025[31]), (IEA, 2019[32]), (European Investment Bank (EIB), 2024[33]), (Africa Agriculture and Trade Investment Fund, 2025[34]), (Money and Banking, 2024[35])

Incentive-based instruments directly reduce the financial burden of investing in sustainable activities, often without requiring repayment. By effectively lowering the cost of capital and operating expenses, these incentives make it more feasible for SMEs to experiment with new solutions, scale up their green initiatives, and transition toward more sustainable business models. Incentive-based instruments can come in the form of:

through instalments or recurring payments, particularly for projects that require long-term investment and maintenance. The funding can also cover external consultancy services and other technical support for SMEs that need to adopt green technologies and practices.

Grants are also important complements to other financing instruments as part of hybrid or blended financing solutions (see above) to incentivise provision and uptake of such financing. In this context grants can be used to: provide technical support such as covering project preparation and implementation costs (e.g. coaching or energy audits); subsidise interest rates or guarantee fees in combination with loans or guarantee instruments; reduce investment costs for the financing recipients such as SMEs; and provide capital rebates to create incentives to reach certain objectives like energy efficiency standards (rebates increase with energy savings as confirmed by energy audits).

Some examples of incentive-based instruments are included in Box 4.3. In Austria, for instance, SMEs can access grants to cover machinery investment costs or consulting services and employee trainings for the implementation of energy management systems. In Slovenia, SMEs can receive grants for advisory services to conduct product life cycle assessments, which help identify environmental impacts and potential green investment needs (see case study from the Slovenian Enterprise Fund in Annex A)

Tax incentives are provided by governments to help reduce the financial burden for SMEs investing in environmentally sustainable technologies. These incentives can include tax credits, deductions, or accelerated depreciation. As mentioned in the introduction, since these instruments are generally not used or implemented by public financial institutions they are not further elaborated on in this report.

Box 4.3. Examples of incentive-based instruments

Grants and subsidies

Austria: The public promotional bank Wirtschaftsservice (aws) offers grants to help SMEs implement energy management systems. The grants can cover external consultancy services, employee trainings, and investments for the required technology. The grants are awarded on a first-come, first-serve basis and can go up to EUR 50 000 of which up to 50% can be used for consultancy services and training costs and 30% for capital investments. The projects should be completed within one to two years.

Slovenia*:* The Slovenian Enterprise Fund offers a **Voucher for Integrated Environmental Impact Assessment** to support SMEs in transitioning to a more sustainable business model. The funding for this advisory service facilitates the implementation of Life Cycle Assessments (LCA), which evaluate the environmental impacts arising throughout a product's life cycle. Funding goes from EUR 3 000 up to EUR 9 999.99.

Türkiye: TÜBİTAK (Türkiye's Scientific and Technological Research Council), in collaboration with the **World Bank**, offers support to SMEs with the transition to greener practices. The **Climate-informed and Green Innovation Technology Extension Program** offers grants to SMEs to cover external consulting services in areas such as green technology solutions, capacity analysis and business roadmap preparation. Grant support is offered for a maximum of 6 months and TÜBİTAK covers 90% of the costs, up to TL 210 000 (USD 11 340 and EUR 5 660 equivalent)

Sources: (aws, 2025[36]), (Interreg Europe, 2025[37]), (TÜBİTAK, 2025[38]).

Sustainability-linked instruments tie the financing terms (e.g. interest rates or payment schedules) to an SME's performance against predefined sustainability-related targets. Unlike green instruments—which often require the proceeds to be used for a specific green project—sustainability-linked instruments measure overall improvements in sustainability metrics (for example, reductions in carbon emissions, energy use, or waste) across the entire business. By rewarding SME adopters with better financing conditions as they meet or exceed sustainability goals, these instruments encourage a broader integration of sustainable practices into day-to-day operations, rather than focusing solely on a single green investment. Common sustainability-linked instruments for SMEs include:

Sustainability-linked loans provide debt financing that is linked to improvements in pre-defined sustainability-related key performance indicators. An example of this kind of support includes the Industrial Bank of Korea's ESG Successful Management Loan, offering reduced interest rates to SMEs that demonstrate improvements in their sustainability performance (see case study from the IBK, Korea in Annex A). In Denmark, SME farmers can obtain a 10-30% interest rate reduction based on their sustainability score in farming practices (see Box 4.4).

Box 4.4. Examples of sustainability-linked instruments for adopters

Sustainability-linked loans

Brazil: Banco do Brasil, in collaboration with the World Bank, provides sustainability linked loans to SMEs through the **Brazil Climate Finance Project**. SMEs can obtain financing for investments in low carbon technologies and equipment. The project also provides accompanying technical assistance, helping SMEs in implementing climate mitigation plans and accessing carbon credit markets. The USD 500 million project is expected to lead to emission reductions of up to 90 million tonnes of CO_2 equivalents by 2030.

Denmark: SME dairy producers are encouraged to adopt green practices through **EIFO**'s **sustainability-linked loans**. This industry-led initiative uses the climate check model of the Danish Dairy Board (FarmAhead), developed by Arla, as a basis, allowing farmers to use the associated tool to assess the environmental impact of their farming practices. Based on their performance across key sustainability indicators such as feed efficiency, land use, protein efficiency, and others, farmers receive a score that EIFO uses to determine financing conditions. Farmers with a score above the national average qualify for interest rate reductions in the range of 10% to 30%.

Japan: The **Development Bank of Japan (DBJ)** offers **Sustainability-Linked Loans (SLLs)** to SMEs, with loan terms structured around the company's performance in achieving sustainability-related performance targets (SPTs). These targets are set by the SME and typically include objectives such as reducing CO_2 emissions, improving energy efficiency, and pursuing other green initiatives that align with environmental goals. The terms of the loan, such as interest rates or repayment conditions, are directly tied to the SME's progress toward meeting these sustainability targets. SMEs participating in the programme are required to provide a mid-term report to DBJ, demonstrating their achievements in relation to the set SPTs. If the SME successfully meets or exceeds its sustainability targets, the loan terms are adjusted favourably, often resulting in lower interest rates or better financing conditions. In addition to the financial support, DBJ provides non-financial services to SMEs through its engagement dialogue, where the DBJ assists SMEs in setting SPTs and implementation through visualising sustainability management.

Korea: the **Industrial Bank of Korea** offers the **ESG Successful Management Loan** to SMEs, with programme, the interest rate is reduced based on the SME's ESG performance, with reductions ranging from 1% for "top-tier" SMEs, 0.5% to those rated as "excellent", and 0.3% for those rated as "good." The loan also includes free ESG assessment and consulting services, provided by the Korean Chamber of Commerce and Industry to help businesses improve their sustainability practices.

Sources: (EIFO, 2024[39]), (Ministry of the Environment, 2022[40]), (World Bank, 2022[41]), (DBJ, 2025[42]).

Green trade finance includes financing instruments which reduce risks for importers and exporters involved in the trade of green goods, technologies, and services. It facilitates sustainable trade by offering tools such as green letters of credit, sustainability linked trade loans and supply chain financing among others. For example, the Climate Smart Programme from the International Finance Corporation offers trade finance instruments to SMEs trading goods related to renewable energy or energy efficiency. The programme provides guarantees for trade finance instruments such as letters of credit or advance payment guarantees. Furthermore, Singaporean SMEs can benefit from extended payment terms for buyers and preferential rates for suppliers of green goods and services under the Green and Sustainable Trade Financing Programme (see Box 4.5). The EBRD supports SMEs in accessing green supply chain finance by partnering with banks to offer risk-sharing and working capital support, as well as grants and advisory services (see case study from the EBRD in Annex A).

Box 4.5. Examples of green trade finance for adopters

Singapore: DBS Bank is incentivising green trade and supply chain opportunities through its **Green and Sustainable Trade Financing** programme. Within this programme, DBS Bank is offering various trade financing instruments to reduce payment risk, such as banker's guarantees, and letters of credit. In addition to risk mitigation, DBS Bank provides direct financing for green trade through solutions like accounts payable financing and accounts receivable financing (see Glossary). Furthermore, the programme includes green supply chain financing, which facilitates extended payment terms for buyers and allows suppliers to access funds at preferential rates.

International: The **Climate Smart Trade Programme** by the **International Finance Corporation (IFC)** promotes the trade of climate-focused goods and services. It builds on the Global Trade Finance Program by offering guarantees to financial institutions for trade-related payment obligations, thus reducing risks and facilitating new trade opportunities. The programme provides price incentives or extended tenors for green goods and services. Guarantees come in various forms, including letters of credit, trade-related promissory notes, and advance payment guarantees, among others (see Glossary). Eligible goods include those related to renewable energy and energy efficiency. Since 2010, the IFC has supported more than USD 2.4 billion in trade deals.

Supply chain finance

International (IFC): The **Global Supply Chain Finance Programme (GSCF)** from the **IFC** provides financing to SME suppliers who are operating both in domestic, as well as international markets. With partnering financial institutions, the programme specifically focuses on promoting green supply chain finance amongst SME suppliers. One such example is a collaboration between the IFC and **Citi,** targeting Mexican SMEs with a total funding of USD 2 billion. Emerging suppliers benefit from improved working capital through being able to convert their receivables into cash and financing open account transactions without the need for collateral. The programme further offers complementary non-financial advisory support to SME suppliers to enhance their ability to access financing.

International (EBRD): The **Sustainable Supply Chain Solutions Framework** by the **EBRD** is making green supply chain financing more accessible to SMEs. Through this programme, the EBRD provides risk-sharing arrangements to partnering banks that offer supply chain financing to large corporations and their SME suppliers. One notable example is a joint program with **Citi**, which supports the Finnish technology company Metso Outotec and its SME suppliers in Turkey. The EBRD has contributed EUR 25 million to this initiative. In addition to financing, the programme promotes sustainability through grants from the Cooperation Fund between the EBRD and Turkey. These grants reward SME suppliers that meet specific emission reduction targets, further incentivising environmental responsibility. The programme also helps SME suppliers access working capital more efficiently, enabling timely financing. Beyond financial support, it provides non-financial assistance through the Advice for Small Businesses program, which helps SMEs adhere to ESG standards and implement sustainable practices

Sources: (IFC, 2025[43]), (DBS, 2025[44]), (IFC, 2025[45]), (EBRD, 2023[46])

Performance-based financing instruments such as Energy Performance Contracts (EPCs) align payments or incentives with the actual environmental performance achieved—often measured in energy savings or emission reductions. In an EPC, a service provider (such as an energy service company) implements efficiency improvements at an SME's facility, and the SME's repayment or fees are determined by the verified energy savings generated. This approach removes much of the financial risk from the SME adopter of energy efficiency technologies, as the SME only pays for improvements that demonstrably reduce energy consumption and costs, ensuring that sustainability investments are directly tied to measurable outcomes.

Market-based instruments like green bonds and carbon credits leverage market mechanisms to channel investment into environmentally beneficial projects. Green bonds raise capital for sustainability-related initiatives at potentially more favourable terms, while carbon credits assign a monetary value to emission reductions, allowing SME adopters to generate revenue from lowering their carbon footprint or purchase credits to offset their emissions. Green bonds, and bonds in general, are not very commonly used by SMEs directly but these instruments can be leveraged by public and private financial institutions, including multilateral development banks, to raise dedicated capital from investors for financing SMEs' green transition, which can then be deployed via different other instruments highlighted here. For example, the World Bank Green Bond programme raises funds from fixed income investors to enable additional lending for green SME projects. Since its inception in 2008, over USD 19 billion equivalent have been raised, across more than 220 bonds in 28 currencies.

4.2. Non-financial support for adopters

Non-financial support is vital for SME adopters in the green transition, as it helps them overcome knowledge gaps, build capacity, and implement sustainable practices effectively. The pairing of non-financial and financial support is relatively common. Non-financial support in particular can address some of the following barriers:

- **Lack of awareness and knowledge:** Many SMEs are unaware of the potential economic and environmental benefits of greening their operations, as well as the specific technologies or processes available to help them achieve sustainability goals. For instance, 63% of small businesses cite lack of skills and knowledge as a barrier to climate action (SME Climate Hub, and practices. Non-financial support can help SMEs understand how sustainability aligns with cost-savings, profitability and long-term resilience. By clarifying the business case for greening, public entities can thus encourage SMEs to see these investments as opportunities rather than costs. In a study mapping capacity-building needs of SMEs to engage in climate action in the Middle East and North Africa Region, 35% of SMEs stated that training and information on climate change background are important (UNFCC, 2023[48]).

Awareness gaps are also a major challenge for SME sustainability measurement and reporting. Some of the key challenges faced by SMEs in this space include limited understanding of sustainability concepts as well as material issues due to lack of specialised staff, limited awareness and understanding of sustainability reporting standards and limited knowledge and experience with sustainability data collection and measurements, among others. Furthermore, SMEs often also lack awareness of the benefits from sustainability reporting and see it rather as a cost or burden. Finally, even when there are tools and support available to SMEs to help with sustainability measurement and reporting, awareness and knowledge gaps can interfere in their utilisation by SMEs.

- **Technical capacity gaps:** Even when SMEs are aware of the benefits from investing in sustainability, they often lack the internal expertise or skills to evaluate and implement appropriate green solutions. This is especially true for micro and small enterprises with limited staff and resources. This is also a key challenge for sustainability measurement and reporting. In a 2025 global survey, 55% of SMEs reported that they would like to get policy support aimed at upskilling staff to take climate action (SME Climate Hub, 2025[49]). Public support in the form of training programs, advisory services, and access to technical experts can help SMEs build the capacity needed to adopt and effectively use relevant technologies and processes and to close capacity gaps for sustainability reporting.
- **High perceived costs and uncertainty**: As noted in the previous chapter, the upfront costs of adopting sustainable practices can appear prohibitive to SMEs whilst the returns on these investments may seem uncertain. About half of SMEs perceive the high cost of green technologies as the primary barrier to adopting more sustainable practices (International Chamber of Commerce, 2024[50]). Non-financial support can reduce these perceived barriers by providing relevant information including cost-benefit analyses, audits, and case studies or fora for knowledge exchange where SMEs can learn about the financial and environmental payoffs of adoption.
- **Administrative and regulatory complexity**: SMEs also face challenges in navigating the complex landscape of environmental regulations, certifications, and reporting requirements, with the complexity of administrative procedures cited among the key barriers to adopting green practices (European Commission, 2024[4]).. Public institutions can simplify this process by providing advisory services, clear guidelines, and easy-to-use compliance tools. These resources can help SMEs understand their obligations and reduce the administrative burden of meeting these obligations.
- **Limited access to markets and networks:** SMEs may lack the connections needed to integrate into green supply chains or access sustainable markets. They may struggle, for example, to identify reliable technology providers, financial partners, or customers seeking sustainable products and services. Public initiatives like matchmaking platforms and trade fairs can help SMEs establish these critical connections.

Table 4.2. Common non-financial support programmes for SME adopters

Support programme	Description	Examples
Awareness campaigns and training programmes	Workshops, seminars and training sessions to help SMEs understand the benefits of greening and aid in implementing sustainability management practices	• Tools to assess and measure their sustainability performance • Sustainability assessment services which enable SMEs to identify gaps in

		their sustainability management • Educational sessions on the economic benefits of implementing sustainability measures
Technical assistance programmes	Hands on assistance through assessments and consulting services on technical aspects of greening	• Conducting environmental impact assessments or energy audits • Quantification tools to measure carbon footprint
Standards and certification support	Guidance and simplification of process to obtain certifications and standards in the form of advisory services, workshops and resources	• Subsidised certification programmes • Simplified documentation requirements • Tools which measure eligibility for obtaining certifications
Sustainability reporting tools	Tools which enable SMEs to measure their sustainability performance and facilitate their reporting	• Automated data reporting tools • Data aggregators and portals

Public entities can address these challenges and externalities by offering relevant informational, technical and capacity building support. Common vehicles for the provision of such support include:

Awareness campaigns and training programmes. Awareness campaigns and training programs play a critical role in helping SME adopters understand the benefits of demonstrating their sustainability performance, transitioning to greener practices and the specific steps required to achieve sustainability goals. Public and private organisations can conduct trainings, workshops and seminars, tailored to SMEs on topics such as energy efficiency, waste reduction, and sustainable supply chain practices. These initiatives not only raise awareness of environmental and financial benefits but also build the skills needed to implement green technologies and processes effectively. In Chile, for example, BancoEstado offers greening support to SMEs through guides and training services, as well as matchmaking services, directing SMEs to relevant financial support avenues (see Box 4.6). Singaporean SMEs can access capacity-building services through the ESG Ready Programme, offering tailored support across five pillars, depending on the ESG readiness level of the SME (see case study on Singapore in Annex A).

Box 4.6. Examples of awareness campaigns and training programmes for SME adopters

Chile: The public development bank **BancoEstado** has introduced the **Green World** Programme, designed to empower SMEs in adopting sustainable practices. The programme provides guidance on the benefits and costs of implementing green technologies. Additionally, it facilitates connections with partner support programmes to help SMEs implement sustainability projects, showcasing available financial support instruments.

Sweden: The public development bank **Almi** offers comprehensive sustainability support to SMEs through guidance, training, and capacity-building initiatives. The bank organises workshops and programmes aimed at enhancing SMEs' knowledge and expertise in sustainability practices. Additionally, Almi provides a sustainability assessment service, helping businesses identify areas for improvement and develop strategies to enhance their environmental performance.

Singapore: DBS Bank, in partnership with the government agency **Enterprise Singapore**, has launched the '**ESG Ready Programme'** to equip SMEs with the tools and knowledge needed to strengthen their sustainability capabilities. The programme offers training, advisory services, and tailored support across five pillars to help SMEs understand and adopt environmental, social, and governance (ESG) practices. It focuses on guiding SMEs in developing and implementing effective sustainability strategies, as well as providing access to DBS' comprehensive suite of sustainable financing solutions. The complementary Sustainability Accelerator Tool enables SMEs to assess their current level of sustainability, providing them with recommendations on which pillar to engage in.

Sources: (Banco Estado, 2024[51]), (almi, 2025[52]), (DBS, 2025[53])

Technical assistance. Technical assistance provides hands-on, expert support to SME adopters, helping them navigate the complexities of transitioning to greener operations. This could include advice on selecting and implementing energy-efficient equipment, redesigning production processes to reduce waste, or integrating renewable energy solutions into their operations. This can also provide support. Technical advisors can also assist SMEs in conducting environmental impact assessments or creating customised sustainability roadmaps. Such assistance ensures that SMEs not only adopt sustainable practices but do so in a cost-effective and impactful manner, minimising risks and maximising long-term benefits. Box 4.7 outlines examples of technical assistance programmes. Indian SMEs can participate in the Green Pathways E-Series, to gain access to reports, case studies and tools to support their greening initiatives. Similarly, SMEs in Japan can benefit from consulting services provided by the Shoko Chukin Bank to assist them in their decarbonisation efforts (see case study on Japan in Annex A).

Box 4.7. Examples of technical assistance programmes for SME adopters

Technical assistance

Australia: SMEs in Canberra can participate in the government's **Sustainable Business Program** to receive technical advice across four areas, including energy, transport, waste and water. Under the programme, SMEs can receive a free on-site assessment from technical experts and unlock access to funding options.

India: The **Small Industries Development Bank of India (SIDB)** is supporting SMEs with sustainability through its **Green Pathways E-Series,** a thematic knowledge initiative designed to guide SMEs on specific low-carbon paths. It offers an expansive suite of knowledge products: expert commentaries, thematic reports, practical case studies, and toolkits for de-risking finance in areas like solar, EVs, energy efficiency, and circular-economy adoption. Collectively, these resources help SMEs navigate financing and implementation of sustainable solutions.

Japan: the state-owned SME development bank **Shoko Chukin Bank** provides **decarbonisation management consulting services** to its SME clients. This includes capacity-building support, such as calculating and visualising emissions and formulating emission reduction targets. The service also offers technical assistance for developing transition plans, to obtain certifications such as the Science Based Targets Initiative (SBTI). A business matching service is also included in the programme, through for example connecting SMEs with relevant renewable energy generation partners.

Morocco: The **EBRD** offers capacity building support to Moroccan SMEs involved in developing and deploying green technologies through its **Green Economy Financing Facility**. The Green Technology Selector is an online tool helping SMEs identify which green technologies are eligible for financing. Expert advice is provided by external consultants on identifying additional investment opportunities and evaluating the effectiveness and sustainability of proposed solutions.

Europe: The **SME Green Skills HUB**, a project which was co-funded by the **European Commission**, offers training modules to SMEs for integrating the Sustainable Development Goals (SDGs) into their business models and operations. The platform connects trainers and mentors with SMEs, offering a framework with a standardised methodology to trainers to ensure consistency across implementation. SMEs can access a tool which assesses their competences on SDG implementation, as well as guidelines and best practices.

International: The **ASEM SMEs Eco Innovation Center** (ASEIC) provides technical support to SMEs on achieving carbon neutrality. Specifically, it supports SMEs in supply chains to manage their greenhouse gas emissions through guidelines and a quantification tool. Additionally, it aids SMEs to establish and implement greenhouse gas reduction goals through consulting programmes in collaboration with local partner companies.

International: The **Green Industry Platform**, under the **United Nations Industrial Development Organization (UNIDO)** and the **Green Growth Knowledge Partnership (GGKP)** have jointly developed the **I-GO Assistant,** helping SMEs identify opportunities to enhance sustainability within their operations. This tool enables SMEs to self-assess their current resource efficiency and circular economy status. The SME then receives tailored recommendations based on their results, and access to relevant support services to further implement sustainability improvements.

International: The **SME Climate Hub** provides measurement tools that help SMEs calculate their carbon footprint. In partnership with **Equipoise and Emitwise**, SMEs can choose between a comprehensive carbon calculator, which quantifies emissions across Scope 1, 2, and 3, and a supply chain calculator, which focuses specifically on Scope 3 emissions within an SME's supply chain.

Conducting energy audits

The **National Development Bank of Czechia** (NRB) is providing technical assistance to SMEs for implementing energy-saving projects in buildings through the **New ELENA programme.** This initiative supports SMEs in adopting measures such as insulation, window replacements, and cooling system upgrades, among others, to improve energy efficiency and reduce emissions. The programme covers up to 90% of project preparation costs, including feasibility studies, energy audits, and investment planning, leaving SMEs responsible for only 10% of the remaining costs. The previous ELENA project in Czechia led to 40 GWh of energy savings and a 24,000-tonne reduction in CO_2 emissions. The project is co-financed by the EU's InvestEU Advisory Hub.

Ireland: The **Sustainable Energy Authority of Ireland** provides support to SMEs on conducting energy audits through the **Support Scheme for Energy Audits (SSEA).** This scheme provides a voucher with expert advice on how to improve and implement energy efficiency measures.

UK: The **Department for Business and Trade** is offering expert advice on energy efficiency through its **SME Energy Efficiency Scheme (SMEES).** The programme combines a grant with technical support on conduct energy audits and identifying ways to save energy. Resources include online tools and workshops.

Sources: (ACT Government, 2021[54]), (I-GO, 2025[55]), (ASEIC, 2025[56]), (SME Climate Hub, 2025[57]), (Shoko Chukin Bank, 2024[58]), (NRB, 2024[59]), (SEAI, 2025[60]), (UK Government, 2022[61]), (SME Green Skills Hub, 2025[62]), (EBRD, 2025[63]), (SIDBI, 2025[64]).

Support with standards and certifications. Attaining sustainability standards and certifications can be a significant barrier for SME adopters due to limited resources or expertise. Public and private entities can provide support by offering subsidised certification programs, guiding SMEs through the compliance process, or simplifying the documentation requirements. Certifications such as ISO 14001 or energy efficiency labels help SMEs gain credibility, access new markets, and align with larger buyers' sustainability requirements. Supporting SMEs in meeting these standards helps them gain access to and remain competitive in green supply chains and contribute to broader environmental goals. Canadian SMEs can

Box 4.8. Examples of support with standards and certifications, knowledge sharing networks and peer learning

Belgium: Cluster Tweed, supported by the **regional government of Wallonia**, helps to connect businesses, research institutions, and public authorities to foster collaboration and innovation in green technologies. The cluster provides SMEs with access to technical expertise, funding opportunities, and collaborative projects that help them develop and scale up environmentally friendly products and sustainable solutions. It also offers networking opportunities, market access, and helps SMEs find partners and customers in the green sector.

Canada: The **Business Development Bank of Canada (BDC)** offers technical assistance to help SMEs obtain a **B-Corp certification**, with a benchmark tool on B-Corp eligibility that firms can use to gauge their alignment to social/environmental objectives.

Netherlands: the **Versnellingshuis Circulaire Economie** (Acceleration House for the Circular Economy) is an initiative from the **Dutch Enterprise Agency (RVO).** The knowledge hub focuses on accelerating the transition to a circular economy by supporting SMEs and entrepreneurs in their efforts to reduce waste, increase resource efficiency, and adopt circular models. It provides advice, networking, and collaboration opportunities, as well as connecting businesses with public and private partners to help them scale circular economy solutions.

Europe: The **European Cluster Collaboration Platform** offers a comprehensive knowledge-sharing hub through its **Green Cluster Collaboration** initiative. This platform connects SMEs, clusters, and business networks across Europe to foster collaboration, innovation, and the development of sustainable solutions. By facilitating the exchange of tools, best practices, and insights, the hub enables SMEs to advance their greening efforts and transition to more sustainable business models. The platform also provides SMEs with access to funding opportunities, expertise, and strategic partnerships, empowering them to develop and scale eco-friendly products and services.

Sources: (European Cluster Collaboration Platform, 2025[65]), (Wallonie, 2025[66]), (BDC, 2025[67]), (RVO, 2024[68])

Knowledge-sharing networks and peer learning. Knowledge-sharing networks and peer learning platforms create opportunities for SME adopters to learn from each other's experiences and best practices in sustainability. These networks can be organised as online forums, industry associations, or regional workshops, enabling SMEs to exchange insights on challenges, solutions, and innovations. By connecting SMEs with similar goals and challenges, these networks accelerate the diffusion of sustainable practices and create a supportive ecosystem for ongoing improvement. Some examples are outlined in Box 4.8. Dutch SMEs who are developing circular economy models can access networking opportunities and matchmaking services to explore collaboration opportunities through an initiative launched by the Dutch Enterprise Agency.

Sustainability reporting. Non-financial support spanning the different categories above is being increasingly offered to SMEs to address the challenge of sustainability performance measurement and reporting which are critical for accessing green and sustainable finance (OECD, 2025[69]). Some critical areas of support include: provision of calculators and tools that can aid SMEs in calculating their carbon footprint or measure other types of sustainability-related metrics that they need to report on; offering standardised reporting templates; provision of relevant institutional and other infrastructure that can facilitate automated data sharing to reduce SMEs' reporting burden; creation of data aggregator and reporting portals that can help SMEs generate sustainability reports that can be shared with many different stakeholders (see Box 4.9). The Danish Business Authority has launched a pilot which aims to automate sustainability reporting practices for SMEs across Europe, significantly reducing administrative burdens (see case study on Automating Sustainability Reporting in Annex A). Capital Markets Malaysia has developed standardised ESG reporting templates, offering step-by-step guidance on sustainability reporting for SMEs across the ASEAN region (see case study from Capital Markets Malaysia in Annex A).

Box 4.9. Tools and support for SME sustainability reporting

Calculators for SME reporting

Denmark: The **Danish Business Authority** in collaboration with the **Danish Energy Agency** have launched a digital carbon footprint calculator (**the Climate Compass**), which is targeted at SMEs. With the Climate Compass, SMEs can access a free, authoritative tool to calculate their emissions in compliance with the GHG-protocol that is continuously updated by the Danish authorities with the newest available data. Additionally, the Climate Compass enables companies to forecast their emissions over a ten-year period and offers guidance in setting emission reduction targets that are in line with the Science Based Targets Initiative (SBTi) and the Paris Agreement.

France: Bpifrance and the **French Agency for Ecological Transition (ADEME)** provide a so-called "**climatometer**," a free tool which allows SMEs to calculate their environmental footprint. SMEs obtain an individual diagnosis assessing climate impacts and recommendations for climate actions they can take.

Industry-led initiatives in venture capital, such as **Invest Europe, ESG_VC** and **VentureESG** highlight an increasing trend of sustainable investing in venture capital. These programs provide advanced frameworks for investors to assess and manage financed emissions, helping to integrate environmental, social, and governance (ESG) considerations into investment decisions. For SMEs and start-ups, these initiatives offer critical access to capital for developing green technologies. ESG_VC, for example, assists start-ups in tracking and improving their ESG performance by providing a free benchmarking tool and hosting training sessions to share best practices. Invest Europe published an updated reporting template in 2024 for private equity and venture capital general and limited partners to incorporate ESG considerations into their operations. The template is aligned with regulatory reporting requirements in the EU and uses a proportional approach, adapting reporting across three stages (minimum, recommended and full reporting), depending on the maturity level of the portfolio companies.

The SME Climate Hub offers practical tools for SMEs such as a **Business Carbon Calculator** as well as educational resources on creating credible transition plans and accessing sustainable finance. The SME Climate Hub recently launched a web-based reporting tool that facilitates climate-related data reporting by SMEs. The reporting tool is aligned with the Carbon Disclosure Project (CDP) and has three main components: reporting on annual GHG emissions, listing actions taken to reduce business and value chain emissions, and monitoring on progress achieved. The SME Climate Hub partners with governments to tailor its products to specific markets and organise awareness raising campaigns. It has done this in a few G20 countries including India, the UK and the US. It has also launched regional campaigns in the Latin America and Caribbean region as well as Middle East and North Africa.

Automating and streamlining data reporting

Denmark: The **Danish Business Authority** is currently implementing a project on **Automated Sustainability Reporting** that aims to automate key company processes related to data collection and management, sharing of sustainability-related information, as well as the digitalisation of businesses' sustainability reporting. This initiative is piloting several key components, including the establishment of a common infrastructure for open data exchange, the development of standardised digital data formats (such as those for the VSME and GHG emissions), and the creation of a standardised data model. This model will be tested and used by private sector actors to streamline sustainability accounting processes. Additionally, Denmark has begun collaborating with other Nordic countries to advance the adoption of automated sustainability reporting across the region.

Germany: The **German Sustainability Code** was developed as a digital tool in 2011, providing companies with a standard to report their sustainability performance. It acts as a management tool, enabling companies to identify material matters as well as developing sustainability strategies and actions. Its digital dimension enables companies to communicate their sustainability performance to their key stakeholders in an accessible way. The tool is free of charge and currently in the process of being updated by the **Federal Ministry for Economic Affairs and Climate Action** to align itself with CSRD. A modular approach will be adopted, providing reporting support to both entities who are required to report under the CSRD and those voluntarily reporting. This will include translating CSRD requirements into simple language and offering free training courses and information services on CSRD reporting to companies, including SMEs.

Singapore: The **Monetary Authority of Singapore (MAS)** developed **Project Greenprint,** a public/private partnership to develop a technology platform that streamlines the collection, access, and use of climate and sustainability data. MAS has also partnered with the United Nations Development Programme (UNDP) and the Global Legal Entity Identifier Foundation (GLEIF) to develop digital sustainability credentials for SMEs and to simplify the ESG reporting process for MSMEs to generate ESG data credentials that can be housed in MSMEs' Legal Entity Identifier (LEI) records. The initiative is currently piloting the inclusion of Scope 1 and Scope 2 emissions data in LEIs.

The Nordics: The **Nordic Accountant Federation (NAF)** created in 2021 a simplified sustainability reporting framework tailored to SMEs, the **Nordic Sustainability Reporting Standard**. The framework was a streamlined version of the GRI reporting standards for large entities, covering all three ESG dimensions. The initiative has since evolved to fully align itself with the previous VSME exposure draft framework of January 2024. With this alignment, the NSRS has transitioned from being a standalone reporting standard to a tool and guidance framework, aligning with its objective of supporting the development of one common European standard. The tool consists of a streamlined reporting template that SMEs can use to comply with the VSME.

UK: Alongside a coalition of public and private stakeholders, the **British Business Bank** is supporting the implementation of **Project Perseus**, an initiative that is piloting a solution enabling the direct provision of data on SMEs' electricity consumption from utilities to financial institutions with SMEs' consent. The pilot architecture developed by this project uses smart meter data to simplify Scope 2 reporting for enterprises by enabling the sharing of these data from energy providers to financial institutions and other relevant stakeholders, with the consent of the enterprise. The solution will be piloted with several financial institutions within a sandbox setting in the early part of 2025.

ASEAN: Capital Markets Malaysia, an affiliate of the Securities Commission Malaysia, has developed the **Simplified ESG Disclosure Guide** for SMEs that are part of international supply chains. The guide offers SMEs a streamlined reporting template in the form of an Excel sheet, which is user-friendly and enables easy data entry that can then be passed onto relevant partners. It provides further sector-specific reporting guidance with additional datapoints. The support tools are provided in multiple languages to increase accessibility. Guides are available for SMEs in Malaysia and across the ASEAN region.

Aggregating data for easier reporting

France: The **Ministry of the Economy and Finance of France** and the digital services incubator (beta.gouv) developed the **RSE Portal,** which provides businesses with a streamlined process to understand and comply with their Corporate Social Responsibility (CSR) and ESG obligations. Upon registration, businesses gain access to a personalised dashboard where they can further refine their criteria and manage their obligations effectively. Businesses can also use the Portal to conduct the so called BDESE (Economic, Social and Environmental Database) reporting, whereby they can fill out relevant forms and be directed to appropriate reporting platforms (e.g. Egapro index, transition plans, etc.).

Greece: The **Hellenic Development Bank** has recently launched their **ESG Tracker**, an online platform that captures the progress of businesses in meeting ESG criteria. The programme is freely accessible and provides firms with a real-time self-assessment and a tool to report on their sustainability progress. The platform aligns itself with international indicators from the Global Reporting Initiative, the Sustainability Accounting Standards Board, the Task Force on Climate Related Disclosures, and the Carbon Disclosure Project as well as national standards used by the Athens Stock Exchange.

Streamlining SME sustainability reporting

International: The **OECD Platform on Financing SMEs for Sustainability** is advancing efforts on fostering convergence in SME sustainability reporting. By mobilising key stakeholders, including financial institutions, standard setters and SME representatives, it is working to foster convergence in SME sustainability reporting across jurisdictions. The OECD has issued a Guidance Note on fostering convergence in SME sustainability reporting, providing a core set of sustainability indicators and metrics for the development of SME sustainability reporting frameworks, as well practical guidance on how to develop and implement such frameworks (Kuzmanovic, Koreen and Honegger, 2025[2]).This initiative seeks to streamline the reporting process across jurisdictions, enabling better alignment and greater transparency in sustainability practices among SMEs.

Sources: (OECD, 2025[69]), (Klimakompasset, 2025[70]), (Bpifrance, 2025[71]), (Invest Europe, 2025[72]), (ESG_VC, 2025[73]), (VentureESG, 2025[74]), (SME Climate Hub, 2025[75]), (Deutscher Nachhaltigkeits Kodex, 2025[76]), (MAS, 2021[77]), (NSRS, 2025[78]), (Icebreaker One, 2025[79]), (Gouvernement francais, 2025[80]), (HDB, 2025[81]), (SEDG, 2025[82])

References

ACT Government (2021), *Sustainable Business Program*, https://www.climatechoices.act.gov.au/policy-programs/sustainable-business-program. [54]

Africa Agriculture and Trade Investment Fund (2025), *About the Fund*, https://www.aatif.lu/objective-of-the-fund.html. [34]

Almi (2025), *Green loan from Almi*, https://www.almi.se/en/loan/green-loan/. [12]

almi (2025), *This is how Almi can assist you in your sustainability efforts*, https://www.almi.se/en/business-development/sustainable-development/this-is-how-almi-can-assist-you-in-your-sustainability-efforts/. [52]

ASEIC (2025), *Support for Carbon Neutrality among SMEs in Member Countries*, http://aseic.org/business_introduction/sme_intro.php. [56]

Asian Development Bank Institute (2018), *Managing Credit Risk and Improving Access to Finance in Green Energy Projects*. [8]

aws (2025), *aws Energie & Klima*, https://www.aws.at/aws-energie-klima/. [36]

Banco Estado (2024), *BancoEstado lanza programa Mundo Verde MiPyme para apoyar la transformación energética de micro, pequeñas y medianas empresas*, https://www.bancoestado.cl/content/bancoestado-public/cl/es/home/inicio---bancoestado-corporativo/noticias/sala-de-prensa-2024--. [51]

Banco Português de Fomento (2025), *Linha de Crédito para a Descarbonização e Economia Circular*, https://www.bpfomento.pt/pt/pt/catalogo/linha-de-credito-para-a-descarbonizacao-e-economia-circular/. [21]

BancoEstado (2025), *Electromovilidad MiPYME*, https://www.bancoestado.cl/content/bancoestado-public/cl/es/home/home/productos-/impacto-verde/impacto-verde-mipyme---bancoestado-empresas/electromovilidad---impacto-verde-bancoestado-mipyme.html#/. [11]

BDC (2025), *Get a green certification for your business*, https://www.bdc.ca/en/articles-tools/sustainability/climate-action-centre/get-green-certification-for-business. [67]

BGK (2025), *Ecological credit*, https://www.bgk.pl/male-i-srednie-przedsiebiorstwa/efektywnosc-energetyczna-i-oze/kredyt-ekologiczny/. [31]

Bpifrance (2025), *Climatomètre*, https://evenements.bpifrance.fr/jour-e-2021/content/climatometre. [71]

Bpifrance (2025), *Garantie Développement Vert*, https://www.bpifrance.fr/catalogue-offres/garantie-developpement-vert. [28]

Clean Energy Finance Corporation (2015), *CEFC helps small businesses cut energy bills and boost performance*, https://www.cefc.com.au/media/107419/cefc-factsheet_smallbusiness_lr.pdf. [13]

DBJ (2025), *DBJ Sustainability Linked Loans with Engagement Dialogue*, https://www.dbj.jp/en/service/sustainability_rating/sll/overview.html. [42]

DBS (2025), *DBS ESG Ready Programme*, https://www.dbs.com.sg/sme/sustainability/esg-ready-programme. [53]

DBS (2025), *Green and Sustainable Trade Financing*, https://www.dbs.com.sg/corporate/sustainability/green-and-sustainable-trade-financing. [44]

Deutscher Nachhaltigkeits Kodex (2025), *New in 2025: Free support for CSRD-compliant sustainability reporting*, https://www.deutscher-nachhaltigkeitskodex.de/en/. [76]

EBRD (2025), *Morocco*, https://ebrdgeff.com/morocco_facilities/. [63]

EBRD (2023), *EBRD and Citi launch sustainable supply chain finance programme with Metso Outotec*, https://www.ebrd.com/news/2023/ebrd-and-citi-launch-sustainable-supply-chain-finance-programme-with-metso-outotec.html. [46]

EIB Group (2024), *EIB Group support offer for the agriculture sector*, https://www.fi-compass.eu/sites/default/files/publications/EIB%20Group%20support%20offer%20for%20the%20agriculture%20sector.pdf. [26]

EIFO (2024), *EIFO will provide cash benefits to green dairy farmers*, https://www.eifo.dk/viden/nyheder/eifo-vil-give-kontante-fordele-til-groenne-maelkeproducenter/. [39]

ESG_VC (2025), *Welcome to ESG_VC*, https://www.esgvc.co.uk/. [73]

European Bank for Reconstruction and Development (2025), *About GEFF*, https://ebrdgeff.com/about-seff/. [15]

European Cluster Collaboration Platform (2025), *Green Transition Support*, https://www.clustercollaboration.eu/green. [65]

European Commission (2024), *SMEs, resource efficiency and green markets (Eurobarometer October 2024)*, https://europa.eu/eurobarometer/surveys/detail/3221. [4]

European Investment Bank (2024), *EIB and Deutsche Leasing support green transformation of small businesses and mid-caps*, https://www.eib.org/en/press/all/2024-064-eib-and-deutsche-leasing-support-green-transformation-of-small-businesses-and-mid-caps. [17]

European Investment Bank (EIB) (2024), *Norway: Nordic businesses to get €190 million green-investment*, https://www.eib.org/en/press/all/2024-462-nordic-businesses-to-get-eur190-million-green-investment-boost-as-eib-group-and-norwegian-dnb-bank-asa-team-up-in-first-of-its-kind-deal-for-region. [33]

European Investment Fund (EIF) (2025), *Financing sustainable businesses and green investment*, https://sustainabilityguarantee.eif.org/. [27]

G20SFWG (2024), *Implementing Sustainability Reporting - Draft Policy Note. OECD contribution to the G20 Sustainable Finance Working Group (SFWG) 9-10 July 2024.*. [1]

Gobierno de Mexico (2025), *FIRA*, https://www.gob.mx/fira. [29]

Gouvernement francais (2025), *Portail RSE*, https://portail-rse.beta.gouv.fr/. [80]

HDB (2025), *ESG Tracker by HDB*, https://esgtracker.hdb.gr/en/home/. [81]

Hellenic Development Bank (2025), *Green Co-Financing Loans*, https://hdb.gr/en/green-co-financing-loans/. [23]

Icebreaker One (2025), *Perseus*, https://ib1.org/perseus/. [79]

IEA (2019), *The Slovak Energy Efficiency and Renewable Energy Finance Facility (SLOVSEFF III)*, https://www.iea.org/policies/795-the-slovak-energy-efficiency-and-renewable-energy-finance-facility-slovseff-iii. [32]

IFAD (2025), *Inclusive Green Financing*, https://www.greenclimate.fund/project/fp183. [24]

IFC (2025), *Global Supply Chain Finance (GSCF)*, https://www.ifc.org/en/what-we-do/sector-expertise/trade-and-supply-chain-finance/global-supply-chain-finance#:~:text=The%20Global%20Supply%20Chain%20Finance,with%20domestic%20and [45]

IFC (2025), *Global Trade Finance Program (GTFP)*, https://www.ifc.org/en/what-we-do/sector-expertise/trade-and-supply-chain-finance/global-trade-finance-program. [43]

I-GO (2025), *I-GO Assistant*, https://igosolution.org/form/i-go-questionnaire. [55]

Industrial Development Corporation (2025), *AFD GREEN ENERGY FUND*, https://www.idc.co.za/afd-green-energy-fund/. [22]

International Chamber of Commerce (2024), *Unlocking sustainable finance for SME The $789 billion green growth opportunity*. [3]

International Chamber of Commerce (2024), *Unlocking sustainable finance for SMEs: The $789 billion green growth opportunity*. [50]

Interreg Europe (2025), *Life Cycle Assesment (LCA) Voucher Scheme*, https://www.interregeurope.eu/good-practices/life-cycle-assesment-lca-voucher-scheme-0. [37]

Invest Europe (2025), *Driving European growth in 2024-29*, https://www.investeurope.eu/. [72]

Klimakompasset (2025), *Klimakompasset*, https://klimakompasset.dk/klimakompasset/auth. [70]

Kreditanstalt für Wiederaufbau (2025), *Nachhaltiges ERP-Globaldarlehen Leasing*, https://www.kfw.de/inlandsfoerderung/Unternehmen/Energie-und-Umwelt/F%C3%B6rderprodukte/Nachhaltiges-ERP-Globaldarlehen-Leasing-(249)/. [16]

Kuzmanovic, M., M. Koreen and G. Honegger (2025), *OECD Guidance Note on Fostering Convergence in SME Sustainability Reporting*, https://www.oecd.org/en/publications/oecd-guidance-note-on-fostering-convergence-in-sme-sustainability-reporting_d95a25de-en.html. [2]

MAS (2021), *Project Greenprint*, https://www.mas.gov.sg/news/media-releases/2023/mas-launches-digital-platform-for-seamless-esg-data-collection-and-access. [77]

Ministry of the Environment (2022), *Green Bond and Sustainability Linked Bond Guidelines*, https://www.env.go.jp/content/000128193.pdf. [40]

Money and Banking (2024), *SME D Bank supports "clean energy" by providing "SME Green Productivity" loans*, https://en.moneyandbanking.co.th/2024/130797/. [25]

Money and Banking (2024), *TCG joins with SME D Bank to guarantee SME Green Productivity loans up to 40 million baht each*, https://moneyandbanking.co.th/en/2024/122647/. [35]

Nacional Financiera (2025), *Eco Crédito Sustentable*, https://www.nafin.com/portalnf/content/financiamiento/eco-credito-sustentable.html. [14]

National Development Bank Czechia (2025), *Energ*, https://www.nrb.cz/en/produkt/energ/. [9]

Nordic Development Fund (2025), *Green Guarantee Facility*, https://www.ndf.int/media/project-files/green_guarantee_facility_english_october_2017.pdf. [30]

NRB (2024), *NRB launches New ELENA advisory to support more energy saving projects*, https://www.nrb.cz/en/nrb-launches-new-elena-advisory-to-support-more-energy-saving-projects/. [59]

NSRS (2025), *What is NSRS?*, https://nsrs.eu/about-nsrs/. [78]

OECD (2025), *OECD Platform on Financing SMEs for Sustainability*, https://www.oecd.org/en/about/programmes/oecd-platform-on-financing-smes-for-sustainability.html. [69]

OECD (2022), *Financing SMEs for Sustainability: Drivers, Constraints and Policies*, https://www.oecd.org/en/publications/financing-smes-for-sustainability_a5e94d92-en.html. [7]

OECD (2021), *No net zero without SMEs: Exploring the key issues for greening SMEs and green entrepreneurship*, https://www.oecd-ilibrary.org/energy/no-net-zero-without-smes_bab63915-en. [5]

RVO (2024), *Versnellingshuis Nederland Circulair*, https://www.rvo.nl/onderwerpen/versnellingshuis. [68]

SEAI (2025), *Energy audits*, https://www.seai.ie/grants/business-grants/energy-audits. [60]

SEDG (2025), *Simplified ESG Disclosure Guide (SEDG)*, https://sedg.capitalmarketsmalaysia.com/. [82]

Shoko Chukin Bank (2024), *Integrated Report 2024*, https://www.shokochukin.co.jp/english/about/company/report/2024/pdf/ir24_all.pdf. [58]

SIDBI (2025), *Green Pathways E-Series*, https://www.sidbi.in/en/green-pathways-e-series. [64]

Small Business Britain (2024), *Small Business, Green Growth*. [6]

Small Industries Development Bank of India (2025), *Financing Schemes for Sustainable Development*, https://www.sidbi.in/head/uploads/other_loans_document/3.%20Financing%20Schemes%20for%20Sustainable%20Development.pdf. [10]

SME Climate Hub (2025), *Calculate your business emissions, https://smeclimatehub.org/start-measuring/*, http://aseic.org/business_introduction/sme_intro.php. [57]

SME Climate Hub (2025), *Report your progress*, https://smeclimatehub.org/report-your-progress/#:~:text=The%20SME%20Reporting%20Tool%20helps,websites%2C%20or%20shared%20with%20stakeholders. [75]

SME Climate Hub (2025), *SME Climate Hub Small Business 2025 Survey*, https://smeclimatehub.org/the-sme-climate-hub-survey/. [49]

SME Climate Hub (2023), *Small Business Climate Action, 2023 Survey*, https://smeclimatehub.org/sme-climate-hub-survey-2023/. [47]

SME Green Skills Hub (2025), *Supporting the implementation of the SDGs in SMEs through VET*, https://smegreenskillshub.eu/. [62]

Sustainability Victoria (2025), *Environmental Upgrade Finance*, https://www.sustainability.vic.gov.au/energy-efficiency-and-reducing-emissions/in-a-business/finance-energy-upgrades-in-you-business/environmental-upgrade-finance-for-business. [19]

TÜBİTAK (2025), *1831 Climate-informed and Green Innovation Technology Extension Program*, [38]

U.S Department of Energy (2025), *Property Assessed Clean Energy Programs*, https://www.energy.gov/scep/slsc/property-assessed-clean-energy-programs. [18]

UK Government (2022), *SME Energy Efficiency Scheme (SMEES)*, https://www.gov.uk/business-finance-support/sme-energy-efficiency-scheme-smees. [61]

UNFCC (2023), "Mapping Study of the Capacity Building Needs and Gaps of SMEs to Engage in Climate Action in the MENA Region", https://unfccc.int/sites/default/files/resource/MENA_SME%20Report_English.pdf. [48]

VentureESG (2025), *Driving the adoption of ESG*, https://www.ventureesg.com/. [74]

Wallonie (2025), *Cluster TWEED*, https://clusters.wallonie.be/tweed/en. [66]

World Bank (2024), *Türkiye Green Industry Project*, https://projects.worldbank.org/en/projects-operations/procurement-detail/OP00278529. [20]

World Bank (2022), *Brazil Climate Finance Project*, https://projects.worldbank.org/en/projects-operations/project-detail/P178888. [41]

Notes

[1] As noted in Chapter 1, tax incentives are not included in the in-depth analysis of this report as the focus is on instruments and programmes that are usually implemented by public financial institutions or equivalent actors.

[2] EBRD is an international financial institution that supports the development of market-oriented economies and private enterprise across Central and Eastern Europe, Central Asia, the Southern and Eastern Mediterranean, and some parts of Sub-Saharan Africa, focusing on sustainable and inclusive growth.

5 Lessons learned and good practices in the provision of financial and non-financial support to SMEs

This chapter synthesises key observations, trends, and common features across green financial instruments and support programmes for SME innovators, enablers, and adopters. It highlights lessons learned from the design and implementation of these initiatives and identifies success factors that contribute to their effectiveness. By drawing on evidence from diverse programmes, the chapter provides insights to guide the development of targeted support mechanisms that enhance SMEs' ability to advance the green transition.

Building on the mapping of relevant financing and non-financial support instruments, a wide range of examples from across OECD and non-OECD economies, and a series of in-depth case studies, the previous three chapters showcase how public support can help SME innovators, enablers and adopters in boosting their contribution to the green transition. This chapter summarises key observations, trends and common features across these instruments and support programmes. It further provides insights on lessons learned and success factors identified in the analysed case studies (see Table 5.1 and Annex A).

It is important to note that the majority of programmes under study are novel and have not yet been subject to a formal evaluation. Insights and lessons learned are, therefore, based on available quantitative and qualitative information. Other elements, such as default rates for most of the guarantee and direct lending programmes, are not available.

Table 5.1. Overview of case studies

Geographical Scope	Provider	Programme	Financing instrument / Non-financial support
Instruments for SME innovators			
Canada	Business Development Bank of Canada (BDC)	The Climate Tech Fund II	Equity and quasi equity financing
Finland	Business Finland	Flexible Energy Systems (FES)	R&D Grants
India	SBI Ventures	Neev II Fund	Equity financing
Malaysia	SME Bank Malaysia and Central Bank of Malaysia	High Tech & Green Facility (HTG)	Concessional loans
Asia	Asian Development Bank (ADB) Ventures	ADB Ventures	Equity and quasi-equity financing
Instruments for SME enablers			
Denmark	Export and Investment Fund of Denmark (EIFO)	Green Accelerator	Supply chain financing
Moldova	Organization for Entrepreneurship Development (ODA)	Credit Guarantee for Renewable Energy Producers	Guarantee
Africa and Asia	Netherlands Enterprise Agency (RVO)	Energy Enterprise Coach	Business development services
Southern Africa	International Climate Initiative, REEEP	SOARING (Southern African Renewable Energy Investment and Growth) Programme	Market access programme
Instruments for SME adopters			
Australia	Sustainability Victoria	Environmental Upgrade Finance	Property-linked loans
Czech Republic	National Development Bank of the Czech Republic (NRB)	Energ programme	Green loans
Denmark	Danish Business Authority (DBA)	Automated Sustainability Reporting	Sustainability reporting support
Japan	Shoko Chukin Bank	Decarbonisation Management Consulting Services	Technical assistance programme
Korea	Industrial Bank of Korea (IBK)	ESG Successful Management Loan	Sustainability linked loans
Malaysia	Capital Markets Malaysia (CMM)	Simplified ESG Disclosure Guide (SEDG)	Sustainability reporting support
Mexico	Nacional Financiera (NAFIN)	Eco Sustainable Credit Programme	Green loans
Singapore	DBS Bank	ESG Ready Programme	Support programme and sustainable financing
Slovenia	Slovenian Enterprise Fund (SEF)	Life Cycle Assessment (LCA) Voucher	Grant
Norway, Sweden, Denmark, Finland	European Investment Bank (EIB) and DNB Bank ASA	EIB's Green Synthetic Securitisation financing initiative in the Nordics	Green synthetic securitisation

EU27, Iceland and Norway	EU (InvestEU programme) and the European Investment Fund (EIF)	InvestEU Sustainability Guarantee and green equity support instruments	Green guarantees
International	European Bank for Reconstruction and Development (EBRD)	Supply Chain Solutions Framework	Green trade finance

5.1. Key trends and features in financial support for SME greening

Policymakers and other public actors have a broad spectrum of instruments at their disposal to support SME sustainability. These range from grants and risk financing for innovators, to sector-specific and revenue-based financing for enablers, and green loans, guarantees, and performance-based financing for adopters. While the structure of these instruments varies, they all aim to expand SME access to sustainable finance while balancing financial risk and viability.

Financing products are becoming increasingly diverse

The study examines a wide range of financing instruments. Many are traditional financing instruments, such as loans, guarantees, and equity funds, that are being redesigned or repurposed to support sustainability objectives. These represent the majority of instruments currently in use. However, there are also many newer instruments being put in place - such as sustainability-linked loans, revenue-based financing, and performance-based contracts – that are designed to specially address sustainability-related constraints as well as objectives. These are typically less widespread, and many are still at an exploratory stage.

There is a growing interest from policymakers in aligning SME financing with sustainability goals and expanding the range of instruments available to support the green transition. While traditional mechanisms such as loan guarantees and concessional financing remain central to SME support, there is increasing recognition that more tailored and flexible instruments may be needed to encourage SMEs to invest in sustainability. As a result, many public financial institutions are experimenting with new financial models. Interviews conducted for this study confirm this trend, with policymakers and financial institutions actively considering additional instruments to further support SME greening, including new risk-sharing mechanisms and sustainability-linked financing solutions.

This growing emphasis on SME financing for sustainability serves a dual purpose: addressing SMEs' access to finance while simultaneously advancing environmental and climate objectives. Many SMEs, particularly smaller and younger firms and innovative firms with a risky business model, struggle to secure affordable financing. Policymakers therefore recognise that green finance initiatives must remain both accessible and practical for businesses across different sectors. At the same time, financial support is clearly tied to sustainability improvements, ensuring that public funds contribute to broader environmental goals. This balance is evident in the design of recent instruments, where public financial institutions are integrating risk-sharing mechanisms, sustainability performance criteria, and technical assistance.

Many programmes are implemented through financial intermediaries

Banks, venture capital funds, and other financial institutions are indispensable partners in most public instruments and play a crucial role in mobilising capital, assessing risk, and scaling up sustainable finance.

Risk-sharing and capital relief measures are often key to increasing financial intermediary engagement. Public-backed guarantees, blended finance structures, and synthetic securitisation (as seen in the EIB Group-DNB model in the Nordics) help de-risk SME lending and free up capital for additional investments.

Similarly, the EU's InvestEU Sustainability Guarantee reduces financing costs for financial intermediaries by covering up to 70% of potential losses on SME green loans, making these investments more attractive.

Public participation in programmes, especially those investing in new and emerging sectors and technologies, play a crucial demonstration role. The Neev II Fund, for instance, helps de-risk nascent climate sectors such as green hydrogen, through taking on early-stage equity stakes and facilitating follow-on investments. As such, the fund sends strong market signals, with its de-risking mechanisms attracting additional capital from commercial banks and institutional investors.

Programmes seek to incentivise the market and develop the financing ecosystem

Defining what qualifies as a sustainable investment for SMEs is complex, and existing reporting frameworks often create additional burdens, compounding the general financial constraints SMEs already face. To address these challenges, targeted incentives for both debt and equity are being deployed to jumpstart the market and build a self-reinforcing cycle of SME participation in sustainable finance. For example, Canada's BDC Climate Tech Fund II and the EU's InvestEU Programme both aim to position SME sustainable finance as a credible, profitable asset class capable of attracting private co-investment.

Over time, these interventions are intended to be phased out, allowing sustainable SME finance to become mainstream and self-sustaining. The long-term goal is to foster market conditions where private financial institutions independently recognise the value of green investments and incorporate them into standard risk assessment and lending practices. By proving the viability and profitability of sustainable SME finance, these programmes aim to catalyse enduring private sector engagement. Furthermore, some policymakers interviewed reported early signs that such support is already influencing the wider ecosystem.

Sustainable finance instruments typically offer more favourable financing conditions

Programmes typically offer concessional terms to SMEs to encourage investment, decrease the risk and lower financial barriers for sustainable investments. This can come in the form of interest rates, as is for example the case of the High Tech & Green Facility in Malaysia, which are substantially below market interest rates. Similarly, the ENERG Programme of the National Development Bank of the Czech Republic provides interest-free loans to SMEs to support energy-efficiency investments.

Favourable financing conditions can also come in the form of longer tenure and reduced collateral requirements as is the case, for instance, of the Eco Sustainable Credit Programme in Mexico. Providing loans which cover full project costs alongside long tenures can also act as an important incentive, especially for green investments with high capital costs, as in the case of the Environmental Upgrade Finance scheme in Australia, which addresses financial barriers of building retrofitting. Additionally risk-sharing arrangements, such as the green synthetic securitisation operation between the EIB and DNB, enable banks to offer below-market interest rates to SMEs, with the EIB partially reimbursing guarantee fees, thereby passing financial benefits directly to SMEs.

Financial institutions are also increasingly designing programmes which reward improvements in SMEs' sustainability performance with more favourable financing conditions. The ESG Successful Management Loan from the Industrial Bank of Korea for example, ties interest rates directly to ESG performance, incentivising SMEs to continuously advance on their sustainability journey.

Financial and non-financial support mechanisms are often used in tandem

Experience from various programmes suggests that financial support alone is often insufficient to drive meaningful adoption of green practices. SMEs lack the technical expertise, strategic capacity or awareness needed to identify the most effective sustainability investments or to meet evolving regulatory and market requirements. As a result, many programmes complement financial support with non-financial support mechanisms. For instance, under the NEEV programme, complementary non-financial support is provided to help companies address weaknesses identified during due diligence, thereby strengthening both their operational and impact performance. The Industrial Bank of Korea's ESG Management Loan combines financial incentives (i.e. interest rate reductions) with ESG consulting services, ensuring that SMEs receive both funding and guidance on improving their sustainability performance.

5.2. Key lessons learned and factors for success

Across the case studies, several success factors can be identified.

Addressing identified market gaps or externalities

Successful programmes have a clear purpose: tackle a specific binding constraint that keeps viable green SME investments from happening. Such constraints include high perceived risk (due to thin collateral, unfamiliarity with new technology, for instance), long payback periods, high transaction costs and information asymmetry problems. In Moldova, for instance, the market failure arose from the observation that certified RES producers, especially start-ups, were credit-constrained by high collateral requirements with existing guarantees not very well suited to make sustainable investments. As a response, the Credit Guarantee for Renewable Energy Producers was introduced. This is a 70% portfolio guarantee with certification as the sole entry requirement, raising caps and removing financial eligibility hurdles. In Malaysia, Capital Markets Malaysia's Simplified ESG Disclosure Guide (SEDG) tackles sustainability reporting constraints by replacing fragmented, variable data requests with standardised, modular templates.

Information and awareness gaps, alongside financial barriers, continue to act as key constraints to SME greening, and programmes are increasingly designed to address them. For example, the Slovenian Enterprise Fund helps SMEs overcome limited knowledge and expertise on conducting sustainability assessments by providing grants for conducting Life Cycle Assessments (LCAs). This reduces the financial burden of such assessments and enables SMEs to identify environmental impacts and improve resource efficiency. Non-financial support programmes also play a key role in addressing knowledge and capacity gaps. In Southern Africa, the SOARING programme addresses limited expertise on sustainability among local financial institutions through technical assistance and capacity-building, improving understanding of clean energy business models and technologies and thereby lowering the perceived risk of financing such projects. In a similar fashion, the Shoko Chukin Bank furthers SMEs' understanding of decarbonisation by offering introductory courses on measuring GHG emissions and developing and implementing emissions reduction strategies.

Unlocking private investments

Programme design should enable the mobilisation of private capital rather than its replacement. Effective schemes do this by:

- **Designing an appropriate risk sharing model.** Banks, equity investors and other financiers can often be encouraged to finance sustainable projects in SMEs if the public sector derisks these investments, for example by first-loss or capped portfolio guarantees, subordinated tranches in blended structures, sustainability-linked pricing or performance premia, and so on. Canada's Climate Tech Fund is a public VC fund that co-invests alongside private investors, typically sharing risk on equal terms and insisting on private participation. Fund I (the predecessor of the more recent Fund 2) estimates show that each public dollar unlocked mobilises around CAD 12 of private

- **Lowering transaction costs.** Streamlining processes such as eligibility checks, due diligence, and reporting can significantly reduce administrative burdens for financing providers and act as a strong incentive for private sector participation. Denmark's Automated Sustainability Reporting (DBA) pilot standardises digital data formats and creates a common exchange layer, so firms and lenders do not have to re-enter the same data, cutting duplication in reporting. Likewise, the EU's InvestEU Sustainability Guarantee Programme provides participating banks with a Sustainability Guarantee Tool, allowing them to quickly verify company and project eligibility against programme requirements
- **Signalling viability**. Public involvement can enhance the credibility of SMEs' projects and demonstrate their market potential to private financiers. By showcasing successful initiatives and organising events which facilitate matchmaking, public actors help financiers identify promising green investment opportunities. The Flexible Energy Systems programme of Business Finland promotes "reference cases" internationally and runs curated workshops and networking events allowing firms that partake in the programme to access private funding (and business partners) more easily, both domestic and internationally. Similarly, the Energy Enterprise Coach from the Netherlands Enterprise Agency organises matchmaking events where SMEs can directly pitch their proposals to investors and financiers to build credibility and reduce perceived risk.

Supporting commercially viable investments

A common feature of many successful programmes is that they support investments that are commercially viable and generate a return on investment. The involvement of private investors is not only highlighted as important because they act as a multiplier, but also because they represent a source of market discipline: banks and equity investors bring underwriting standards, pricing of risk, governance requirements, and ongoing monitoring that help ensure capital flows to viable projects rather than those sustained only by subsidies. Several case study interviews brought across the point that sustainable investments are more durable if they are also sustainable in the commercial sense and that sustainability in the environmental sense should not come at the expense of market viability.

In that respect, it is also important to note that interventions aim to reduce the risk to private investors to a reasonable level, not eliminate it entirely so private actors have a vested interest in the project. In practice this can mean requiring some private co-financing at project level, as in the case of ADB Ventures, which has adopted a co-investment approach for early- and growth-stage companies to mobilise additional funding while keeping private investors financially engaged. Another approach is structuring loss-sharing arrangements, so intermediaries retain exposure. Mexico's NAFIN Eco Sustainable Credit Programme provides guarantees up to 80% for that reason, with part of the risk borne by banks, which also conduct standard risk assessment procedures and decide what projects to finance. Through a green synthetic securitisation, the EIB Group transfers part of the credit risk on DNB's SME loan portfolio, freeing regulatory capital on the condition that it is redeployed into new climate-aligned SME lending. The deal ensures only viable projects are supported via capped first-loss/stop-loss features and relies on DNB's standard underwriting and monitoring.

Balancing potential trade-offs between SME access and impact

Sustainable finance programmes face an inherent tension: ideally, they should be accessible to smaller firms and to enterprises that are not yet leaders in sustainability, since these often have the greatest potential for improvement. At the same time, programmes must safeguard public funds and deliver credible, measurable outcomes. Balancing these goals is difficult. If thresholds are kept high, programmes may achieve verifiable impact but risk excluding smaller or less mature SMEs. If thresholds are lowered to widen participation, take-up increases but the risk of dilution and weaker monitoring also grows.

This tension plays out in both eligibility criteria and due diligence processes. Programmes that adopt a tight-targeting approach—with high performance thresholds and rigorous assessments—tend to prioritise measurable impact and investment quality. Examples include the Neev II Fund in India or Denmark's Green Accelerator, which focus on growth-stage enterprises with scalable solutions. While such approaches deliver strong returns and reduce risk, participation rates are often low; in the case of Neev II, only one in 60–70 applications succeed. Extensive due diligence requirements can also raise costs for both SMEs and financial institutions, with many intermediaries relying on external consultants to manage assessments.

On the other hand, programmes that take a broad audience approach lower thresholds and simplify procedures in order to reach more firms, expand learning effects, and build stronger project pipelines. Mexico's Eco Sustainable Credit Programme, for instance, requires energy audits but has worked to streamline procedures and reduce collateral requirements. ADB Ventures applies a flexible reporting approach, with lighter requirements for early-stage ventures and more rigorous assessments for advanced companies. Similarly, some institutions have begun experimenting with pre-application support, simplified checklists, and digital self-assessments to cut transaction costs for SMEs (see more in section on non-financial support below).

In practice, most programmes do not make a sharp binary choice but instead seek to balance access and integrity. Graduated requirements, clear safeguards, and targeted technical assistance are increasingly used to allow more firms to qualify without undermining credibility. The challenge lies in calibrating due diligence and reporting demands so that they do not exclude the very enterprises—smaller, earlier-stage, or emerging-market SMEs—that are central to the green transition.

Choosing the right intermediaries and partners

Choosing the right delivery partner can be just as important as choosing the instrument. For complex, intermediate finance solutions, it is important to consider intermediaries with the skills, systems, and governance to execute at pace and with integrity. A good illustration is the EIF–DNB green synthetic securitisation in the Nordics, where an experienced commercial bank partnered with a public financier to transfer part of the credit risk on a portfolio of SME loans, freeing up regulatory capital to originate additional green lending. This works only when the intermediary can structure risk transfer to meet regulatory and accounting requirements, run robust SME credit processes, and report use-of-proceeds and impact accurately.

This is also an important consideration for supply-chain financing instruments, where it is useful to have partners who can aggregate demand and set credible standards. The EBRD's Supply Chain Solutions approach shows the power of partnering with anchor buyers. Large purchasers help define eligible measures for their suppliers (e.g. equipment upgrades that meet the buyer's sustainability standard), endorse vendor lists, and sometimes share data for verification. A large part of the success of the programme can be attributed to the involvement of trusted and capable partners.'

Partners can also play a crucial role in strengthening awareness and outreach among SMEs. The Environmental Upgrade Finance scheme in Australia for example, successfully leveraged channel partners through engaging service providers of environmentally friendly building upgrade equipment. These partners promoted the scheme directly as a financing option within their sales processes which supported uptake among SMEs.

In the context of the provision of non-financial support, having the right partners is also critical to ensure strong quality of service delivery, especially in areas where the public financial institution does not have internal expertise. The Canadian BDC Climate Tech Fund II, while not offering direct support to the end beneficiaries, often refers companies to other providers of support on a needs basis and considers the strong connection to the broader (public) eco system as a strong point. Likewise, DBS Bank in Sing is drawing on its connections with platform providers and consulting firms to give SMEs access to expert advice on carbon footprint calculation and the development of decarbonisation strategies.

Beyond technical capacity, the alignment of partners' incentives with programme objectives is also essential, as is ensuring accountability through clear performance metrics. Participating banks in the Supply Chain Solutions Framework from the EBRD who are extending credit must comply with the EBRD Performance Requirements and submit annual environmental and social reports to ensure alignment with programme objectives. In a similar fashion, under the EU's InvestEU Sustainability Guarantee programme intermediaries are required to undergo quarterly documentation and reporting. The European Investment Fund conducts audits and visits to ensure compliance and proper implementation to ensure alignment with programme objectives.

Making outreach an integral part of support

For many SMEs, sustainability is not yet a strategic priority, and even where it is recognised as important, firms often lack relevant knowledge (e.g. on what clean technologies or processes to adopt) or are unaware of available public support programmes. Many programmes, therefore, adopt systematic outreach efforts to bolster SME awareness and uptake. Typical measures include multi-channel communication through banks, sector associations and chambers of commerce, anchor-buyer supplier portals, and regional business support centres. In Slovenia, for instance, the SEF LCA voucher leverages sector associations and local chambers of commerce to disseminate calls and guide SMEs, complemented by 12 regional SPOT one-stop offices that help firms prepare applications and documentation. In Singapore, DBS Bank has started integrating sustainability into its masterclasses for micro and small enterprises to raise awareness on sustainability issues. It also provides networking opportunities with key stakeholders and circulates peer success stories among its SME clients to make sustainability more tangible and actionable.

Strengthening non-financial support for SME investments in greening and uptake of associated financing

Providing financing alone is rarely enough to ensure that SMEs can successfully participate in green transition programmes. Many firms face barriers not only in meeting eligibility requirements but also in managing the administrative and technical demands of applying for and reporting on green finance. Adding advisory services, technical assistance, and simplified procedures can broaden access without compromising standards. Subsidised audits and diagnostics, as well as coaching on ESG and impact reporting, can help SMEs meet verification requirements. At the same time, clear checklists, streamlined forms, and digital self-assessments reduce transaction costs, making it possible for credible applications to come from a much broader set of enterprises.

Several examples illustrate how this approach is being put into practice. In India, the Neev Fund II complements its equity financing with tailored non-financial support to help SMEs address weaknesses identified during due diligence. This improves both operational performance and impact outcomes. In Denmark, the Green Accelerator programme streamlines the application process through an online portal and provides pre-application support for assessing eligibility and preparing strong project proposals, which improves overall programme efficiency. In Czechia, the ENERG Programme was designed to cover up to 80% of the costs of energy assessments, directly reducing the administrative and financial burden on applicants. In Malaysia, the High Tech & Green Facility lowered reporting thresholds for smaller firms, making concessional loans more accessible.

These cases also demonstrate that thoughtful programme design can expand SME access while preserving sustainability objectives. By combining finance with advisory services, capacity-building, and procedural simplification, institutions are not only fostering broader take-up but also enhancing the credibility and effectiveness of SME greening initiatives.

Leveraging digital tools for access, uptake and efficient implementation

Given the novelty of many instruments and the need to manage volume at reasonable cost, programmes increasingly deploy digital tools and portals. Various programmes use digital eligibility checklists, work with a dedicated portal where interested companies can access all relevant information in one place and have fully digitalised the application process. For example, under the EU's InvestEU Sustainability Guarantee, the EIF provides a web-based Sustainability Guarantee Tool and online Green Eligibility Checker to help intermediaries and SMEs pre-assess whether enterprises or projects meet the programme's criteria, with an indicative view of climate impact where applicable. In Slovenia, the e-Voucher portal handles submission and reimbursement entirely online with two-factor digital signatures and electronic contracting, streamlining SME access to the Life-Cycle Assessment voucher. The ESG Ready Programme from DBS Bank in Singapore leverages an online tool, the Sustainability Accelerator Tool, which allows SMEs to self-assess their current sustainability performance to receive tailored recommendations on the most suitable entry point within the modular structure of the programme.

Digital tools also play an increasingly important role in supporting and streamlining sustainability reporting for SMEs (OECD, 2024[1]). This is particularly important for reporting on more complex indicators, which require SMEs to access external data sources and undergo complex calculations. Capital Market Malaysia, for example, is now working on developing a GHG emissions calculator with integrated emission factors, in response to challenges identified among SMEs in calculating their carbon footprint. Other digital initiatives are aiming to simplify SME sustainability reporting through automation processes. The Danish Business Authority for example, is piloting a system that extracts relevant data from both internal and external sources and processes it automatically to enable seamless sustainability reporting for SMEs.

Reducing SME compliance costs by aligning processes and reporting with (inter)national standards

Reporting is generally burdensome for SMEs, so programmes should keep processes simple. At the same time, public authorities still need credible verification that supported activities are genuinely sustainable (and need to apply due diligence procedures that apply to SME policies more broadly). Public bodies can draw on emerging practice from national administrations and international institutions to standardise templates, align criteria with recognised taxonomies, deploy digital portals, and adopt proportional verification.

A case in point is Malaysia's Simplified ESG Disclosure Guide (SEDG), which offers modular templates benchmarked to GRI/ISSB/CDP so firms at different maturities can report once and reuse data. Similarly, the Life Cycle Assessment voucher from the Slovenian Enterprise Fund uses templates which are aligned with ISO 14040/14044 standards to enhance credibility and comparability. Another example is the InvestEU Sustainability Guarantee Tool/Green Eligibility Checker, which lets intermediaries and SMEs test alignment ex-ante, and which could be employed for other programmes at the (sub)regional level across the globe. A further example is Denmark's Automated Sustainability Reporting initiative, which standardises digital data formats and a common exchange infrastructure to cut duplication. The OECD Guidance Note on Fostering Convergence in SME Sustainability Reporting can also serve as a tool to align reporting requirements with the core indicators and metrics used in major international frameworks and standards (Kuzmanovic, Koreen and Honegger, 2025[2]).

Strengthening access and impact through flexibility and adaptability

As noted in the previous section, many green and sustainability-linked SME financing instruments are still taking shape in many jurisdictions, with best practices under development. Programmes are therefore balancing accessibility with accountability. In Czechia, the ENERG Programme has tuned its terms over time, cutting the loan rate from 2% to zero to stay competitive and allowing grants to be applied directly to reduce loan balances, which improved uptake among cash-constrained firms. At EU level, the InvestEU Sustainability Guarantee is rethinking allocation in response to oversubscription, considering ways to prioritise intermediaries that reach underserved borrowers. Finland's Flexible Energy Systems Programme also shows administrative flexibility: it uses studies and calls to shape pipelines and offers feedback and conversion pathways (e.g. redirecting strong but ineligible grant proposals to loan instruments), reducing search and compliance costs without lowering standards.

To ensure evidence-based programmes that evolve, adapt and improve, the establishment of monitoring and evaluation systems is also essential.

Reinforcing and mainstreaming sustainability considerations in the SME financing ecosystem

Successful policies should not only finance individual projects but mainstream sustainable lending practices for SMEs. As a long-term impact, they often aim to strengthen the market infrastructure that enables repeatable, scalable transactions to take place even in the absence of any government intervention. This includes working with intermediaries with relevant expertise and skills so that climate-aligned lending becomes part of standard practices of financial institutions. The EIB/EIF–DNB green synthetic securitisation, which frees regulatory capital on SME portfolios conditional on redeployment into climate projects, is an example of this type of effort. In addition, other avenues to mainstream SME sustainability include:

- Policies that provide taxonomy-aligned eligibility and pre-screening tools can make SME lending for sustainable projects more common. The EU's InvestEU Sustainability Guarantee Programme offers its Sustainability Guarantee Tool, which enables financial institutions to quickly and seamlessly assess SME eligibility.
- Subsidised or standardised energy audits and diagnostics that help identify eligible investments and generate verifiable baselines, such as the ENERG programme in the Czech Republic, allowing financial institutions to quantify the energy-saving impacts of their borrowers.
- Digital reporting and common data formats to cut duplication and improve interoperability. Denmark's Automated Sustainability Reporting initiative standardises data capture and eases the reporting burden, simplifying verification for lenders and encouraging uptake.
- Modular disclosure templates mapped to international standards so that SMEs at different maturities only have to report on their sustainability performance once and can reuse data. Malaysia's Simplified ESG Disclosure Guide (SEDG) offers step-by-step, standardised templates that help SMEs and lenders converge on comparable and consistent information.

5.3. References

Kuzmanovic, M., M. Koreen and G. Honegger (2025), *OECD Guidance Note on Fostering Convergence in SME Sustainability Reporting*, https://www.oecd.org/en/publications/oecd-guidance-note-on-fostering-convergence-in-sme-sustainability-reporting_d95a25de-en.html. [2]

OECD (2024), *Fostering convergence in SME sustainability reporting: A background study*, https://www.oecd.org/en/publications/fostering-convergence-in-sme-sustainability-reporting_ffbf16fb-en.html. [1]

6 Conclusions

This concluding chapter highlights the pivotal role of SMEs in driving the green transition and the importance of public policy in addressing financing gaps and mobilising sustainable investment. It underscores that effective SME greening requires an integrated approach combining financial instruments with non-financial measures that build capacity, reduce risk, and enhance project quality. Drawing on lessons from across OECD and non-OECD countries, the chapter identifies successful practices for crowding in private capital, strengthening delivery mechanisms, and leveraging digital tools to improve access and impact.

SMEs are pivotal to advancing the green transition, yet their contribution is often held back by limited access to appropriate finance. This report highlights the critical role of public policy in closing these financing gaps and mobilising sustainable investment for SMEs. By segmenting SMEs according to their roles as innovators, enablers, and adopters of green practices, it maps a broad spectrum of public financial and complementary non-financial support measures implemented across OECD countries and beyond. This mapping is enriched by a set of in-depth case studies that provide practical lessons for the effective design and delivery of such programmes.

Drawing on the diverse experiences documented throughout the report and in the case studies, several clear lessons emerge regarding how financing and non-financial support can most effectively enable SMEs to pursue greener business practices.

Scaling up financing for SME greening requires an integrated approach that goes beyond capital provision. Public interventions should be designed to target market gaps, such as high perceived risks, long payback periods, and information asymmetries, while ensuring that supported investments are commercially viable and capable of attracting private capital. Risk-sharing mechanisms, concessional terms, and demonstration effects can all help crowd in private financing providers, multiplying the impact of public resources.

Equally important is the provision of non-financial support to lower entry barriers and strengthen the quality of projects. Advisory services, subsidised audits, reporting guidance, and simplified digital procedures can help SMEs meet eligibility and compliance requirements without diluting sustainability standards. Well-designed technical assistance also builds the long-term capacity of SMEs to manage green investments and embed sustainability in their business models.

Programme design and delivery channels play a decisive role. Selecting skilled intermediaries and partners ensures that financing and support are delivered efficiently, transparently, and at scale, while digital tools can reduce transaction costs, improve monitoring, and create stronger pipelines. By reinforcing the broader ecosystem—developing common standards, building institutional capacity, and mainstreaming sustainable lending practices—public finance can ensure that SME greening can be scaled up and accelerated.

Putting these lessons into practice can enable adoption and scaling of similar solutions in countries around the world, adapted to specific local contexts and the needs of SMEs. The OECD Committee on SMEs and Entrepreneurship, and its Platform on Financing SMEs for Sustainability, will continue their efforts to support governments and financial institutions in enabling SMEs to drive the transition to sustainability.

Annex A. Case studies

Case studies of financial and non-financial support for SME innovators:

- Asian Development Bank – ADB Ventures
- Business Development Bank of Canada – Climate Tech Fund II
- Business Finland – Flexible Energy Systems programme
- SBI Ventures Limited – Neev II Fund in India
- SME Bank Malaysia – High Tech & Green Facility

Case studies of financial and non-financial support for SME enablers:

- Export and Investment Fund of Denmark – Green Accelerator programme
- Netherlands Enterprise Agency – Energy Enterprise Coach in Africa and Asia
- Organization for Entrepreneurship Development – credit guarantee for renewable energy producers in Moldova
- Renewable Energy and Energy Efficiency Partnership – Southern African Renewable Energy Investment and Growth Programme

Case studies of financial and non-financial support for SME adopters:

- Capital Markets Malaysia – Simplified ESG Disclosure Guide for SMEs in Supply Chains
- Danish Business Authority – Automated Sustainability Reporting initiative
- DBS Bank – ESG Ready Programme in Singapore
- DNB and the European Investment Bank Group - green synthetic securitisation in the Nordics
- European Bank for Reconstruction and Development – Supply Chain Solutions Framework
- Industrial Bank of Korea – ESG successful management loan
- InvestEU Sustainability Guarantee Programme in the European Union
- Nacional Financiera – Eco Sustainable Credit programme in Mexico
- National Development Bank of the Czech Republic – ENERG Programme, Prague
- Shoko Chukin Bank – decarbonisation management consulting service in Japan
- Slovenian Enterprise Fund – Life Cycle Assessment voucher
- Sustainability Victoria – Environmental Upgrade Finance programme in Australia

Annex B. Glossary

Accounts payable financing: This financing instrument is part of the broader category of supply chain financing that optimise cash flow by enabling suppliers, which can be small businesses, to receive early payment for their invoices, while allowing buyers to maintain or extend their payment terms through the involvement of a financial intermediary. This instrument is similar to reverse factoring in that it is buyer initiated and leverages the buyer's liquidity for financing SME suppliers. The key difference is that the financing goes to the buyer who then uses it to pay suppliers promptly at the agreed payment dates even while benefitting from extended payment terms vis-à-vis the financing providers. This mechanism thus effectively helps SMEs avoid cash flow issues from late payments from buyers. Public financial institutions can facilitate this kind of funding by offering guarantees or concessional rates on AP financing tied to green supply chains.

Accounts receivable financing: This financing mechanism seeks to support SME supplier liquidity by leveraging upcoming payments from buyers (which are part of the SMEs' accounts receivable), but unlike early payment programmes and reverse factoring, it is supplier-driven and relies on the supplier's own creditworthiness to get the necessary financing. Public financial institutions can support SME adopters in obtaining AR financing by de-risking (e.g. through guarantees), or subsidising the financing provided by intermediaries.

Advance payment guarantee: Financing instrument which is issued by a bank or guarantor ensuring that advance payments made by a buyer will be refunded if the supplier fails to deliver the contracted goods or services.

Blended finance: It combines public, philanthropic, and private capital to support projects with environmental impact. Public funds or concessional funding (such as grants, subsidies, or first loss guarantees) are used to absorb risk, to lower investment risks and attract private capital.

Collaborative financing models: Larger buyers or public sector players in supply chains can collaborate with financial institutions, including public financial institutions, to offer supply chain financing solutions to SME suppliers with the objective of incentivising supplier adoption of green practices. Buyers can use their creditworthiness to secure favourable terms for their suppliers, reducing the cost of financing greening investments for SMEs.

Concessional loans: Loans provided at below-market interest rates, often with more favourable terms, such as longer repayment periods or grace periods. These loans are offered to support projects with environmental goals, making it easier for borrowers to access capital.

Convertible debt: A hybrid instrument, classified also under quasi equity instruments, that starts off as a loan but can be converted into equity when a specific milestone is reached. One advantage of such financing is that the conversion terms enable alignment between the interest of lenders and SMEs in that the latter get capital for their risky ventures and lenders get the potential upside of having a stake in a successful venture.

Early payment programmes: Programmes that enable SME adopters to receive funds earlier for their approved invoices, and this can be done through a financial intermediary or the buyer itself. This improves cash flow, helping them invest in sustainable upgrades. These programs also reduce reliance on expensive short-term loans. Public financial institutions can collaborate with larger buyers to subsidize or de-risk early payment programs specifically for SME adopters meeting green criteria.

Equity financing: It provides capital to businesses in exchange for ownership stakes or rights linked to financial performance. Commonly used for SME innovators and start-ups to fund innovation, growth, and expansion.

Green guarantees: Financing instruments that provide a guarantee to lenders or investors, for risk mitigation. These guarantees encourage investment in green initiatives by covering potential losses, enabling SMEs to access funding for green projects.

Green leasing: A financing option where SMEs lease environmentally sustainable assets, like energy-efficient equipment, to reduce high upfront costs and by spreading costs through periodic lease payments. Green leases often include favourable terms or incentives for green solutions and are often provided by private entities with public support in the form of risk sharing mechanisms.

Green letters of credit: They can support SME adopters importing eco-friendly inputs, such as energy-efficient machinery, renewable energy systems, or sustainable raw materials. These instruments provide payment guarantees to exporters, enabling SMEs to confidently source high-quality green products. PFIs can offer subsidized fees for green letters of credit, guaranteeing transactions where SME adopters import sustainable goods.

Green loans: Loans specifically designed to finance projects that have positive environmental impacts, such as renewable energy, energy efficiency, circular economy and sustainable agriculture. These often offer competitive or subsidised financing costs and flexible terms, such as longer repayment periods. They can vary in terms of duration and can be directly provided by public development banks or through intermediary financial institutions.

Green synthetic securitisation: A financial structure in which green assets, such as green loans, are pooled and securitised using credit derivatives, transferring risk to investors while retaining asset ownership. Alternatively, green securitisation can be achieved through use-of-proceeds, i.e. by freeing up capital for new green projects without selling the underlying assets.

Green trade finance: This includes financing instruments which reduce risks for importers and exporters involved in the trade of green goods, technologies, and services. It facilitates sustainable trade by offering tools such as green letters of credit, sustainability linked trade loans and supply chain financing, amongst others.

Incubator and accelerator programmes: Programmes designed to support early-stage start-ups and SMEs by providing resources, mentorship, funding, and networking opportunities to help them grow and scale.

Import financing for sustainable goods: Part of green trade finance, this financing can help SMEs to offset costs associated with importing sustainable materials or technologies, which can often be high. Import financing enables SME adopters to pay for these inputs over time, reducing the upfront financial burden.

Inventory financing for sustainable inputs: Inventory financing, part of the broader category of supply chain finance, allows SMEs to use these green inputs as collateral to access financing from financial institutions, enabling them to spread costs over time while maintaining production. Public financial institutions can create targeted inventory financing programs for SME adopters sourcing certified green inputs, offering concessional rates or guarantees to lower the financial burden.

Mezzanine financing: Financing that combines debt and equity often with flexible repayment and profit participation or warrants. It entails higher risk for investors which is compensated with equity like returns or profit sharing. It is commonly used for later-stage green start-ups that are looking to scale their operations.

Mini bonds: Issuance of debt by SMEs which are pooled together through a securitisation process to attract institutional and private investors. With lower regulatory requirements than traditional bonds, mini bonds are often backed by public financial institutions to enhance creditworthiness and reduce investment risk, enabling SMEs to access capital for green projects.

Performance-based instruments: Financial tools that provide funding or incentives contingent upon achieving specific environmental or sustainability outcomes, such as carbon reduction or energy efficiency. Repayments are based on verified emission reductions or energy savings, reducing financial risk.

Profit participation loans: Loans that link repayment with a certain percent of the SME's profits instead of a fixed interest payment. This reduces the pressure on SMEs in the early stage of growth when the profits may be low or negative as well as during any times of downturn. Incentive alignment is another key benefit from this kind of a financing instrument.

Promissory note: A written commitment by a buyer to pay a specified amount of money to a seller, either when requested or at a predetermined date, in exchange for goods or services delivered.

Property-linked loans: Loans designed to finance environmentally friendly property improvements, where repayment is tied to the revenue or cost savings generated from energy-efficient upgrades or sustainable building features. These loans allow SMEs to invest in green building projects or energy-efficient retrofits, using the property's future savings or increased value as collateral or a source of repayment. By linking repayment to the property's performance, these loans reduce financial risk for SMEs, making it easier to access capital.

Purchase order financing: When SMEs secure large orders requiring them to use eco-friendly materials or processes, they may lack the upfront capital to fulfil these orders. Purchase order financing, which is part of the broader category of supply chain finance, bridges this gap by providing in advance the financing needed to fulfil green procurement contracts. Public financial institutions can offer purchase order financing tailored to SME adopters working on sustainability-focused orders, particularly those tied to public procurement or supply chains with green mandates.

Quasi-equity instruments: Flexible financing tools that provide capital to businesses in exchange for rights linked to financial performance, such as profit-sharing or the potential for conversion into equity through instruments like convertible debt.

Research and development (R&D) grants: Non-repayable funds provided to SMEs to support innovation and the development of new technologies, products, or processes. These grants help cover the costs of research and experimentation, enabling businesses to advance their solutions without the immediate pressure of repayment.

Revenue-based loans: A debt-financing mechanism where repayments are tied to a percentage of the revenue generated from green projects, rather than fixed installments. This structure allows for more flexibility, reducing the cash flow burden on SMEs.

Reverse factoring: In reverse factoring, the buyers (often large corporations) can initiate early payment to their SME suppliers by working with financial institutions and leveraging their own creditworthiness. This enables buyers to extend payment terms with their suppliers without negatively affecting the supplier's cash flow. For suppliers, this enables earlier access to payments obtained from the financial institution on the basis of the approved invoices from the buyers. Public financial institutions can encourage reverse factoring arrangements for SME adopters in green supply chains by acting as intermediaries or guarantors.

Subordinated loans: These loans rank below other types of debt in case of bankruptcy but typically offer more flexible repayment terms. As such they are higher risk financing for lenders and often entail higher financing costs, but they enable SMEs to retain full ownership and control of their company.

Supply chain financing: Financing that provides SME adopters with access to affordable and timely capital while encouraging sustainability adoption within supply chains. Supply chain financing can include a wide range of financing programmes that leverage to different degrees the buyers' (often large corporations) credit worthiness or purchasing power to help SMEs get access to more timely financing to address working capital needs or free up finances for investment.

Sustainability linked loans: Loans tied to sustainability performance that serve to incentivise SME adopters to achieve green milestones, such as reducing emissions, improving energy efficiency, or sourcing certified sustainable materials.

www.ingramcontent.com/pod-product-compliance
Lightning Source LLC
LaVergne TN
LVHW060454061126
851857LV00016B/1823